My
Office for iPad®

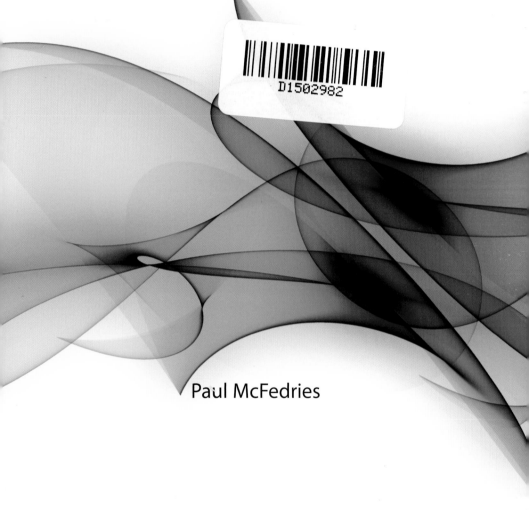

D1502982

Paul McFedries

que®

800 East 96th Street,
Indianapolis, Indiana 46240 USA

My Office® for iPad®

Copyright © 2015 by Pearson Education

ISBN-13: 978-0-7897-4873-7

ISBN-10: 0-7897-4873-8

Library of Congress Control Number: 2014939231

Printed in the United States of America

First Printing: July 2014

Trademarks

All terms mentioned in this book that are known to be trademarks or service marks have been appropriately capitalized. Que Publishing cannot attest to the accuracy of this information. Use of a term in this book should not be regarded as affecting the validity of any trademark or service mark.

Warning and Disclaimer

Every effort has been made to make this book as complete and as accurate as possible, but no warranty or fitness is implied. The information provided is on an "as is" basis. The author and the publisher shall have neither liability nor responsibility to any person or entity with respect to any loss or damages arising from the information contained in this book.

Special Sales

For information about buying this title in bulk quantities, or for special sales opportunities (which may include electronic versions; custom cover designs; and content particular to your business, training goals, marketing focus, or branding interests), please contact our corporate sales department at corpsales@pearsoned.com or (800) 382-3419.

For government sales inquiries, please contact governmentsales@pearsoned.com.

For questions about sales outside the U.S., please contact international@pearsoned.com.

Editor-in-Chief
Greg Wiegand

Senior Acquisitions Editor
Laura Norman

Development Editors
William Abner
Todd Brakke

Managing Editor
Kristy Hart

Senior Project Editor
Lori Lyons

Copy Editor
San Dee Phillips,
Apostrophe Editing
Services

Indexer
Erika Millen

Proofreader
Katie Matejka

Technical Editor
J. Boyd Nolan

Editorial Assistant
Kristen Watterson

Cover Designer
Marc Shirar

Compositor
Bronkella Publishing

Contents at a Glance

Table of Contents

| 3 | **Working with Office for iPad Graphics** | **51** |

| 4 | **Working with Text in Word** | **67** |

About the Author

Paul McFedries is a Microsoft Office expert and full-time technical writer. Paul has been authoring computer books since 1991 and has more than 85 books to his credit, which combined have sold more than 4 million copies worldwide. His titles include the Que Publishing books *Formulas and Functions with Microsoft Excel 2013* and *Windows 8.1 In Depth* (with coauthor Brian Knittel), as well as the Sams Publishing book *Windows 7 Unleashed*. Paul is also the proprietor of Word Spy (www.wordspy.com), a website devoted to *lexpionage*, the sleuthing of new words and phrases that have entered the English language.

Please drop by Paul's personal website at www.mcfedries.com or follow Paul on Twitter at twitter.com/paulmcf and twitter.com/wordspy.

Dedication

To Karen

Acknowledgments

If you re-read your work, you can find on re-reading a great deal of repetition can be avoided by re-reading and editing.

—William Safire

In the fast-paced world of computer book writing, where deadlines come whooshing at you at alarming speeds and with dismaying regularity, rereading a manuscript is a luxury reserved only for those who have figured out how to live a 36-hour day. Fortunately, every computer book *does* get reread—not once, not twice, but *many* times. I speak, of course, not of the diligence of this book's author but of the yeoman work done by this book's many and various editors, those sharp-eyed, virtual-red-pencil-wielding worthies whose job it is to make a book's author look good. Near the front of the book you'll find a long list of those hard-working professionals. However, there are a few folks I worked with directly, and I'd like to single them out for extra credit. A big, heaping helping of thanks goes out to acquisitions editors Loretta Yates and Laura Norman, development editor William Abner, technical editor J. Boyd Nolan, project editor Lori Lyons, copy editor San Dee Phillips, and compositor Tricia Bronkella. A heaping helping of thanks to you all!

We Want to Hear from You!

As the reader of this book, *you* are our most important critic and commentator. We value your opinion and want to know what we're doing right, what we could do better, what areas you'd like to see us publish in, and any other words of wisdom you're willing to pass our way.

We welcome your comments. You can email or write to let us know what you did or didn't like about this book—as well as what we can do to make our books better.

Please note that we cannot help you with technical problems related to the topic of this book.

When you write, please be sure to include this book's title and author as well as your name and email address. We will carefully review your comments and share them with the author and editors who worked on the book.

Email: feedback@quepublishing.com

Mail: Que Publishing
         ATTN: Reader Feedback
         800 East 96th Street
         Indianapolis, IN 46240 USA

Reader Services

Visit our website and register this book at quepublishing.com/register for convenient access to any updates, downloads, or errata that might be available for this book.

Introduction

The history of personal computing is, to a large extent, a story of increasing the mobility of both hardware and data. With the original personal computers, the "personal" part referred not only to the idea of a computer that belonged to and could be used by a single person but also to the fact that, unlike its mainframe and minicomputer predecessors, the PC could be moved from one room to another. Truly portable PCs arrived just a few years later, and the past 30 years or so have seen PCs shrink to what will perhaps be the PC form factor's smallest incarnation: the smartphone.

The smartphone is an amazing invention, but what it offers in terms of mobility it lacks in screen size. Yes, you can use a smartphone to compose an email message, but would you want to use one to compose an essay? Can you imagine trying to put together a budget or build a presentation on a tiny smartphone screen? Fortunately, there's another device available that's nearly as mobile as a smartphone but with a screen size that's closer to a notebook PC. I speak, of course, of the tablet, which just might be the ultimate combination of portability and size (at least until the next newfangled gadget comes along). The iPad (both the Air and the mini), in particular, is light and easy to hold, and has a screen that's big enough for serious work such as word processing, spreadsheet crafting, and presentation building.

Microsoft has seen the usability and portability of the iPad and now offers a suite of apps called Office for iPad. These are scaled-down versions of Word, Excel, and PowerPoint, as well as a separate app for OneNote, that are small enough to fit comfortably on the iPad, but powerful enough to let you perform many of your day-to-day productivity chores.

Office for iPad offers seamless integration with OneDrive, the online storage area that comes with a Microsoft account. This means that you can work on a document on your desktop, save it to OneDrive, and then pick up where you left off by accessing the same document using an Internet connection on your iPad. Saving happens automatically behind the scenes, so you're never in danger of losing your work. No extra equipment is needed because everything—from typing to formatting to inserting images, tables, and charts—happens on the iPad screen and is controlled by finger taps.

Welcome to *My Office for iPad*

This book introduces you to the Office for iPad apps and shows you how to get the most out of them. You will learn how to use the Office for iPad apps, what to expect from them, and what their limitations are. *My Office for iPad* takes you through every feature found in the apps, shows you how to use the apps to collaborate on documents, and even offers a tutorial on using OneDrive. *My Office for iPad* offers you the following:

- It shows you benefits and limitations of the Office for iPad apps and describes best practices for using the apps.

- It details all the available features in the iPad versions of Word, Excel, PowerPoint, and OneNote.

- It gives you enough background on OneDrive to manage Office documents online.

- It offers key information on collaboration, using both the iPad apps and OneDrive.

- It explains key concepts for novice users.

- It offers real-world examples you can relate to.

Sign in to
your Microsoft
account

Create a new
document

Create a new
document from
a template

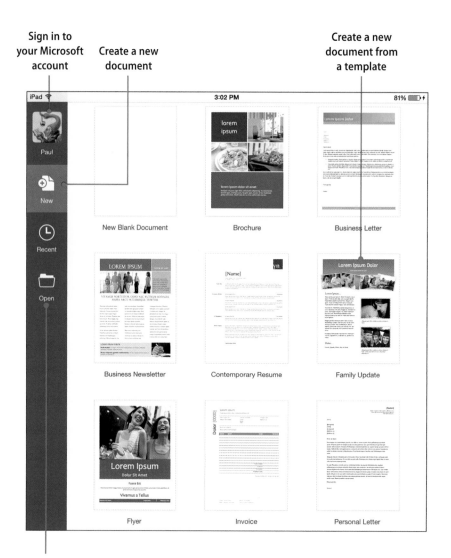

Open an
existing
document

In this chapter, you learn about starting the Office for iPad programs, working with documents, and saving your work.

→ Understanding Office 365 and Office for iPad

→ Taking your first steps with Office for iPad

→ Creating a new document

→ Preserving your work

→ Working with documents

Getting Started with Office for iPad

Most of this book deals with the specific features of the four Office for iPad apps—Word, Excel, PowerPoint, and OneNote—and a bit later you learn all of the most useful and practical techniques that these powerful programs have to offer. However, these programs also have quite a few features in common, and some of these tools and techniques are the most useful and the most important. Sample techniques that fall into these categories include creating documents, saving documents, and duplicating documents.

This chapter takes you through all these techniques, but you begin with an overview of Office 365 and a comparison of the Office for iPad apps with the desktop cousins.

Understanding Office 365 and Office for iPad

We live in a world in which smartphones and tablets garner most of the attention of the technical (and even mainstream) press. This isn't a surprise because technologists and industry insiders have fawned over the latest gadgets for as long as there has been a technology industry. However, gadgets come and go, but one thing has stayed the same over that time: People still need to write, calculate, and present, whether for business or for pleasure.

Microsoft Office is a suite of programs designed to help people do just that. Whether you have a memo to write, a budget to build, a presentation to create, or some notes to jot down, the Office programs have the tools to help you get the job done. Unfortunately, Office is expensive (between $139 and $249, depending on the suite) and difficult to maintain, so most home users have shied away from it.

That is now changing with the introduction of Office 365, which enables everyday folks like you and me to use the Office programs without breaking the bank and without requiring an in-house tech support department.

Learning How Office 365 Works

Office 365 is a subscription-based service that gives you access to Office programs. There are several options for Office 365 subscriptions, but the most popular is Office 365 Home Premium, which offers Word, Excel, PowerPoint, OneNote, Outlook, Publisher, and Access for $10 per month or $99 per year (as of this writing). You're allowed to install these programs on up to five computers, and you can install Office for iPad—a scaled-down version of Office that includes the iPad versions of Word, Excel, PowerPoint, and OneNote—on up to five tablets. Up to five different people can use Office 365, and each gets 20 GB of storage on OneDrive, Microsoft's online file storage service.

To use Office 365, you (and each person who uses Office 365 in your household) need to have a Microsoft account. This is an email address (it can be one of your existing addresses) that you associate with your Office 365 subscription. By signing in to your account on each computer and tablet where you use Office 365, you get immediate access to your Office 365 settings, customizations, and files. This means, for example, that you can work on a document using a desktop Office program at home, save the document to OneDrive, and then continue working on the document when you take your iPad to the local coffee shop.

Automatic Update

Another big advantage of using Office for iPad is that you don't have to worry about upgrades and versions because all this is handled automatically, behind the scenes. This means you'll always be working with the latest version of each app.

Comparing Office for iPad with Desktop Office

In the past, when you wanted to work with a Microsoft Office document, you had two choices: Open the document in its native Office application, which gave you full access to the document and to the application's commands and features, or open the document in a "viewer" application, which allowed you to only read the document. The Office for iPad apps lie somewhere in the middle—that is, they go beyond mere viewers to offer you tools not only for reading Office documents but also for adding and editing data, making for-matting changes, and so on. However, the Office for iPad apps aren't meant to be a substitute for their desktop cousins, so they come with only a relatively small subset of the features found in the desktop versions. For example, in the Excel app, you can build formulas and work with functions, but you can't use data analysis tools such as Goal Seek and Solver.

Editing Requires a Subscription

I should clarify that if you don't have an Office 365 subscription, then the Office for iPad apps are just file viewers, because although anyone can run the apps and open documents, to edit them you need a subscription.

When you begin working with any of the Office for iPad apps, the first thing you notice is that they feel a lot like their respective desktop versions:

- Each Office for iPad app comes with a Ribbon that looks and operates just like the Ribbon in the desktop programs.

- The Ribbon in each Office for iPad app is a scaled-down version of the desktop Ribbon. In most cases, with the Office for iPad Ribbon, you get a Home tab, an Insert tab, a Review tab, and a View tab.

- Within each Ribbon tab in the Office for iPad apps, you get only a subset of the commands found in the equivalent Ribbon tab on the desktop.

- There are contextual tabs in the Office for iPad apps. (There are tabs that appear only when you select a particular object in a document.) For example, clicking inside a table in desktop Word invokes the Table Tools contextual tab with table-related commands, and tapping inside a table in Word for iPad displays the Table contextual tab.

- The Office for iPad apps have a scaled-down version of the Quick Access Toolbar, which appears just above the Ribbon and contains just the Undo and Redo commands.

- The Office for iPad apps File menu is a scaled-down version of the File menu you see in the desktop programs. In fact, the Office for iPad File menu contains just three file-related commands: New, Recent, and Open.

- The content area for each Office for iPad app is similar to that of its desktop cousin, which makes it easier to get up to speed when editing a document using your iPad. For example, the Excel for iPad app comes with the familiar row and column headers, gridlines, sheet tabs, and formula bar (although it doesn't support in-cell editing).

Taking Your First Steps with Office for iPad

If you want to use the Office for iPad apps for more than just viewing your documents, you must sign in or create a Microsoft account, and then use that account to purchase an Office 365 subscription. This book assumes that you have already downloaded the Office for iPad apps from the App Store on your iPad.

Sign In to Your Microsoft Account

Having a Microsoft account means you can save Office documents online in your OneDrive and have your account and app settings follow you from the iPad to the desktop and back. So begin your Office for iPad journey by signing in to your account, if you have one.

1. On your iPad (which needs to be connected to the Internet for these steps), tap the icon of any Office for iPad app to launch that app. The app displays several screens that give you an overview; then the Sign In Now screen appears.

2. Tap Sign In. If you need to create an account instead, see the next section.

3. Type your Microsoft account email address.

4. Tap Next.

5. Type your account password.

6. Tap Sign In.

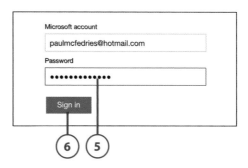

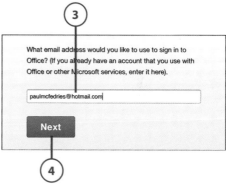

7. Tap an option that determines whether you want to send product information to Microsoft as you use the Office for iPad apps.

8. Tap Continue.

9. Tap Start Using *App*, where *App* is the Office for iPad app you launched in Step 1.

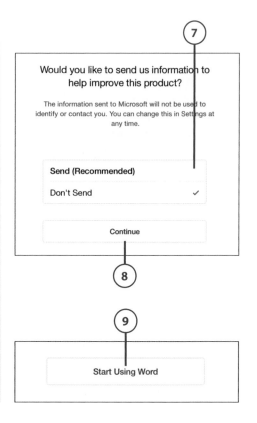

It's Not All Good

Sharing Usage Data with Microsoft

Sending information to Microsoft means sharing data about how you use the Office for iPad apps, as well as statistics that are generated automatically when an app crashes. This data is anonymous and does not include any personal information, so it's safe to share. However, if you elect to share the data and then later change your mind, you can stop the sharing. To do this, tap your iPad's Settings icon, tap the name of the Office for iPad app that has sharing enabled, tap Help Us Improve, and then tap the Send Usage and Crash Data switch to Off.

Create a Microsoft Account

If you don't have a Microsoft account, you need to create one to get the most out of Office for iPad. You can use an existing email address for the account or create a new address.

1. On your iPad, tap the icon of any Office for iPad app to launch that app. The app displays several screens that give you an overview; then the Sign In Now screen appears.

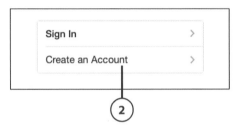

2. Tap Create an Account.

3. Type your first name.

4. Type your last name.

5. Type the email address you want to use.

Creating a New Address

If you don't want to use an existing email address for your Microsoft account, tap Or Get a New Email Address, and then specify the address you want.

6. Type the password you want to use.

7. Select your country.

8. Type your ZIP or postal code.

9. Specify your date of birth.

10. Select your gender.

Tap here if you want to create a new account

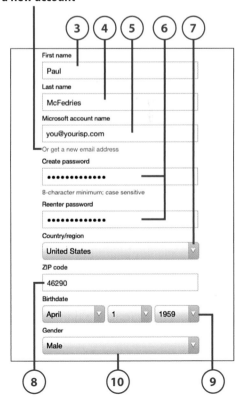

11. Select your phone number country code.

12. Type your phone number.

13. Type the characters your see. This is to prove that you're a real person and not some automated program trying to create the account.

14. Tap Create Account.

15. Type your Microsoft account email address.

16. Tap Next.

17. Type your account password.

18. Tap Sign In.

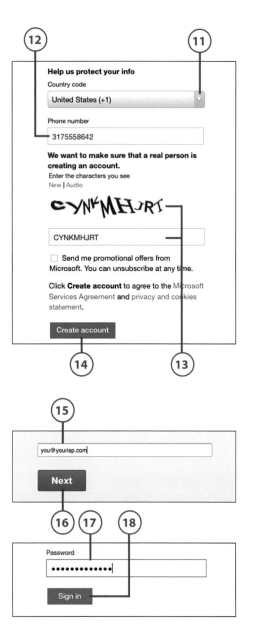

>>>Go Further

YOUR PHONE NUMBER

You need to provide Microsoft with a phone number as a security precaution. If you access your Microsoft account from a new device, Microsoft doesn't know if it's you trying to access the account or some unauthorized person. To make sure, Microsoft doesn't allow access at first. Instead, it sends a text message to the phone number you provided, and you must enter the code from the text message to prove that you're not an intruder.

Purchase an Office 365 Subscription

After you sign in to your Microsoft account, the system checks to see if you have an existing Office 365 subscription. If you don't, particularly if you just created your Microsoft account, then you need to purchase a subscription to use Office for iPad for more than simply viewing documents.

These steps assume you have either signed in to an existing Microsoft account or created a new Microsoft account as described in the previous two sections.

1. Tap Buy Office 365 Home.

2. Tap Buy Now.

3. Type your App Store password.

4. Tap OK.

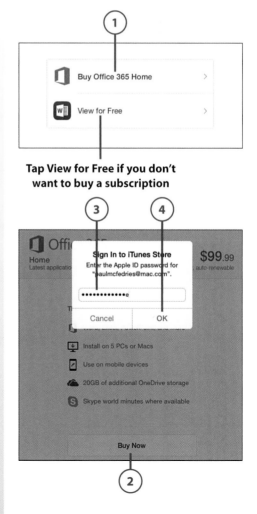

Tap View for Free if you don't want to buy a subscription

5. Tap Confirm.

6. Tap OK.

7. Tap an option that determines whether you want to send product information to Microsoft as you use the Office for iPad apps.

8. Tap Continue.

9. Tap Start Using *App*, where *App* is the Office for iPad app you launched originally.

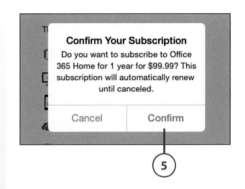

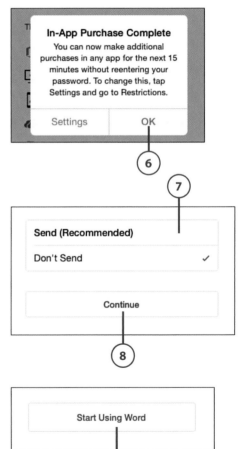

Sign Out of Your Microsoft Account

If someone else will be using your iPad, you might want to sign out of your Microsoft account so that person can't access your online documents and settings.

1. Tap Back.

2. Tap the account icon.

3. Tap your Microsoft account.

Account Icon Picture

The image you see for the account icon is the picture associated with your Microsoft account profile. You learn how to change this picture in Chapter 13, "Learning OneDrive Essentials."

---

4. Tap Sign Out. The app asks you to confirm.

5. Tap Sign Out.

Signing Back In

When you're ready to reconnect to your Microsoft account, tap File, tap Sign In, type your account address and password, and then tap Sign In.

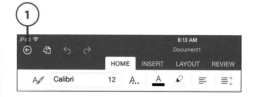

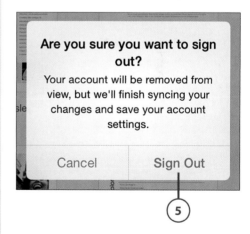

Switch Between Office for iPad Applications

Your iPad supports multitasking, which means you can have more than one Office for iPad app open at the same time. If you run multiple Office apps, you need to know how to switch between them.

1. Double-press the iPad's Home button. That is, you press the Home button twice quickly. The iPad's multitasking screen appears, which displays a list of running apps.

2. Flick left or right to bring into view the thumbnail image of the Office for iPad app you want to use next.

3. Tap the thumbnail image of the app. Your iPad switches to the app.

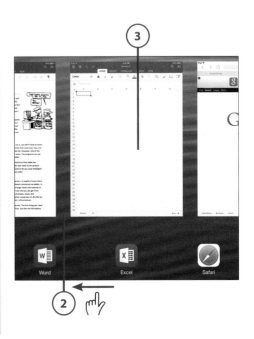

>>>Go Further
SWITCHING APPS WITH GESTURES

You can also switch between running apps by placing four fingers on the iPad screen and then swiping to the left to bring the next app into view. Continue swiping left until you get to the app you want to use. You can also four-finger swipe right to cycle back between the running apps.

If you prefer to use the multitasking screen, instead of double-pressing the Home button, you can also place four fingers on the screen and then swipe up.

Quit an Office for iPad Application

The iPad manages app resources automatically, so you usually do not need to quit an app. However, if an Office for iPad app is no longer responsive, or if you just want to reduce clutter on the multitasking screen, you can quit an app manually.

1. Double-press the iPad's Home button. The iPad's multitasking screen appears, which displays a list of running apps.

2. Flick left or right to bring into view the thumbnail image of the Office for iPad app you want to quit.

3. Tap and drag the thumbnail image of the app up to the top of the screen until it disappears. Your iPad closes the app.

Creating a New Document

To perform work in an Office for iPad app, you must first either create a new document or open an existing document. In this section, you learn about creating new documents.

Although OneNote creates a notebook for you to use as soon as you start the app, the other Office for iPad apps—Word, Excel, and PowerPoint—don't create a new document for you automatically. Instead, if you don't need to open an existing document, then you must create a new document by hand when you launch these apps. In each case, you can either create a blank document that is devoid of data and formatting, or you can create a document from a template, which is a special file that includes prefabricated content and formatting.

>>>Go Further

SAVING TIME WITH TEMPLATES

One secret to success in the business world is to let the experts do whatever it is they are good at. Let the salespeople sell, the copywriters write, and the designers design. If you try to do these things yourself, chances are that it will take you longer and the results will not be as good.

You can apply the same idea to the Office world. Why spend endless hours tweaking the design and layout of a brochure when a professionally designed brochure is just a few screen taps away? I am talking about using *templates*, special documents that come with predefined layouts, color schemes, graphics, and text.

Create a Blank Document at Startup

You can create a new, blank document as soon as you start Word, Excel, or PowerPoint.

1. Start the app you want to use.

2. Tap the blank option, such as Word's New Blank Document icon.

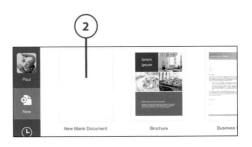

Create a Blank Document After an Office for iPad Application Is Running

If you are already using Word, Excel, or PowerPoint, you can create a new, blank document from within the app.

1. Tap Back.

Saving a New Document
If the document you're currently working on is new and has never been saved, the app will prompt you to save or delete the document. See "Save a New Document" later in this chapter.

---

2. Tap New to display the New tab.

3. Tap the blank option, such as Excel's New Blank Workbook icon.

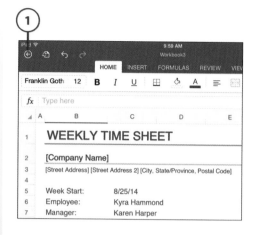

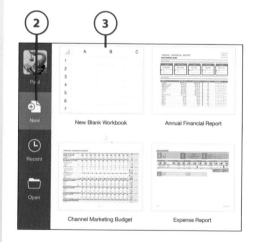

Creating a Document from a Template or Theme

Word and Excel for iPad each come with a few templates that contain preformatted text, images, and other elements that enable you to quickly create great-looking documents such as newsletters, invoices, and budgets. PowerPoint for iPad comes with a few themes, each of which offers preset colors, fonts, and backgrounds for each slide layout.

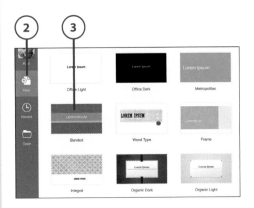

These were all created by professional designers and most are quite striking. Of course, after you create a document based on a template or theme, you can tweak the layout, design, and text to suit your needs.

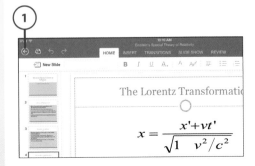

1. Tap Back.

2. Tap New to display the New tab.

3. Tap a template (in Word or Excel) or a theme (in PowerPoint, which is what's shown here).

Preserving Your Work

Losing precious data due to a system crash is a constant, nagging worry for PC users. Why is it such a problem? The main reason is that when you work with a document, your PC takes a copy of the document from the hard drive and loads that copy into memory. This makes it much faster to work with the file, but the downside is that all the data loaded into memory is lost when your PC crashes or loses power. This means that if you've made changes to your document, those changes are lost when the memory is wiped.

This is much less of a problem with Office for iPad. Yes, the apps still load documents into memory either from the iPad's hard drive or from your OneDrive, but the Office for iPad apps have a feature called AutoSave that automatically saves your data as you work. The only time you could potentially lose a great deal of work is when you edit a new document that hasn't been saved, so it's important to save new documents as soon as possible.

Save a New Document

Although you no longer have to worry about saving existing documents with Office for iPad, you must still save new documents. To avoid losing work, you should save a new document either immediately, or as soon as you're sure you want to preserve the document.

1. Tap File to open the File dialog.

2. Tap Name. The Save As dialog appears.

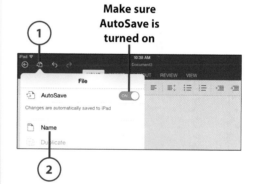

Make sure AutoSave is turned on

Checking AutoSave
While you have the File dialog open, this is a good time to double-check that the AutoSave switch is activated.

3. Type a name for the document.

4. Tap the location where you want the document saved: your OneDrive or your iPad.

5. If you're saving the document to your OneDrive, tap the folder that you want to use to store the document.

6. Tap Save.

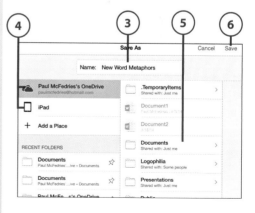

>>>Go Further

FILE NAMING GUIDELINES

The complete pathname for any document must not exceed 255 characters. The pathname includes not only the filename, but also the location of the document, including the drive letter, colon, folder name (or names), and backslashes. The filename can include any alphanumeric character, one or more spaces, and any of the following characters:

~ ` @ # $ % ^ & ( ) _ - + = { } [ ] ; , . '

The filename must not include any of the following characters:

* | \ : " < > ?

Create a Duplicate of a Document

One of the best ways to save time and increase your efficiency is to, as the saying goes, avoid reinventing the wheel. With Office for iPad, this means that if you need to create a document that is similar to an existing document, don't build the new document from scratch. Instead, create a copy of the existing document and then modify the copy as needed.

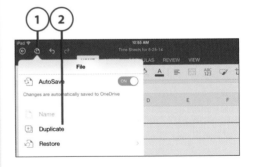

1. Tap File.

2. Tap Duplicate.

3. Type a name for the copy.

File Naming Guidelines

To avoid overwriting the existing document, make sure you select a different folder, specify a different filename, or both.

4. Tap the location where you want the duplicate document saved: your OneDrive or your iPad.

5. If you're saving the duplicate to your OneDrive, tap the folder that you want to use to store the document.

6. Tap Save.

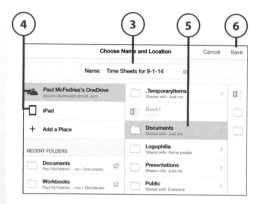

Convert a Document to the Latest Format

Word, Excel, and PowerPoint for iPad can open any document that uses a relatively recent Office file format, which means anything created with Office 97 and later. However, to edit an Office document using the iPad apps, that document must use one of the Office Open XML file formats introduced in Office 2007 (and continued unchanged in Office 2010 and 2013 for Windows and Office 2008 and 2011 for Mac). When you open an older file format, the app prompts you to convert the document to the latest format.

1. Open a document that uses an older Office file format.

2. Tap Convert and Edit to open the Save As dialog.

3. Tap Save. The app converts the document to the latest format.

4. Tap OK.

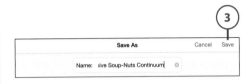

It's Not All Good

Converting Creates a Copy

When Office for iPad converts the document to the latest file format, it creates a copy and leaves the original document untouched. This means it will appear as though you have two documents with the same name. What you actually have is one document (the original) named *something*.doc (to use a Word document as an example) and a second document (the converted copy) named *something*.docx. Office for iPad hides file extensions (the .doc and .docx part of the name), so these two files appear the same, which can be confusing. One way to tell them apart is to examine the icon that appears to the left of each file in the Open dialog. If the icon is the same as the one that appears with the app on the Start screen, then the document uses the latest file format. To avoid this kind of confusion, consider moving the older version of the file to another location.

Working with Documents

You'll spend almost all your Office for iPad time writing, editing, and formatting documents, but you'll also regularly face more mundane document chores, such as opening documents, switching from one document to another, and restoring previous versions of documents. The rest of this chapter takes you through these day-to-day document tasks.

Open a Document

When you launch an Office for iPad app, the program first displays a window that includes a Recent list, which shows the last few documents that you've worked with in the app. You can reopen a document by selecting it from that list. If you don't see the document you want, then you need to use the Open list to select the file.

1. Tap Back.

2. Tap Open to display the Open tab.

3. Tap the location where your document resides: your OneDrive or your iPad.

4. If the document is on your OneDrive, tap the folder that stores the document.

5. Tap the document to open it.

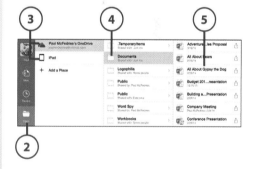

It's Not All Good

Switching Between Documents

One common scenario is to start the process of opening another document, but then change your mind. On a PC or Mac, you'd then cancel the Open dialog box, but the Office for iPad apps fail to offer any such convenience. After you tap Back, the Office for iPad app immediately closes (and saves) the existing document, so there's no simple route to get that document back on the screen if you decide not to open a different document after all. Your only choice is to re-open the previous document.

One consequence of this behavior is that it's not possible to have two (or more) documents open at the same time in the same Office for iPad app. So although it's easy to switch between open documents in the desktop versions of the Office programs, you can't do that in Office for iPad.

Pin a Document to the Recent Tab

The fact that the Office for iPad apps don't allow more than one open document at a time is inconvenient, particularly if you find yourself constantly switching between multiple documents. You can make this a little more convenient by pinning the documents you use most often to the Recent tab, which ensures they're always no more than three taps away.

1. Tap Back.

2. Tap Recent to display the Recent tab.

3. Tap the pin icon next to the document you want to pin.

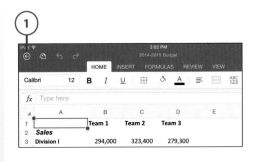

**Pinned documents
always appear in
the Recent tab's
Pinned section**

Restore an Older Version of a Document

If you make a mistake when editing a document, you can quickly reverse that error by tapping Undo. However, what if you notice the error only an hour, a day, or even a week later? In that case, you can restore the earlier version because Office keeps tracks of versions as you create them.

1. Tap File.

2. Tap Restore. The Restore dialog appears.

3. To discard your changes in the current editing session, tap Restore to Last Opened; to restore to an earlier version, tap View Version History Online, instead.

4. Tap a version to display it.

5. Tap Restore.

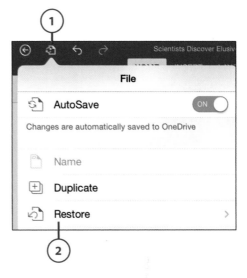

>>>*Go Further*
RESTORING AN OLDER VERSION AS A COPY

Rather than overwriting the current version with a previous version, you can download the earlier version as a copy. To do this, follow steps 1 through 4 and then tap Download. Safari opens the version and briefly displays the Open In bar. (If you miss this bar, tap Reload to display it again.) Tap Open In; then tap Open in *App*, where *App* is the name of the Office for the iPad app associated with the document type. This opens the document as a read-only copy. You can then copy whatever text you need, or tap Save and Edit if you want to make changes to the document.

Apply
styles

Set the text
font and size

Apply text
effects

Align and indent
paragraphs

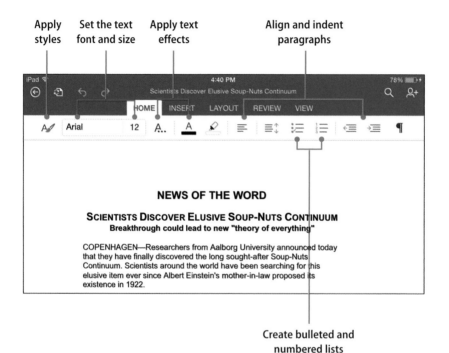

Create bulleted and
numbered lists

In this chapter, you learn various ways to format your Office for iPad documents, including changing the font, creating bulleted and numbered lists, and applying styles.

→ Setting the typeface, type size, and other font effects

→ Building bulleted and numbered lists

→ Working with indentation and alignment

→ Applying styles to document text

→ Clearing formatting

Formatting Documents

One of the consequences of the domination enjoyed by Microsoft Office in the productivity suite market is that people—particularly businesspeople—now have high expectations. That is, because so many users have access to powerful formatting techniques, people expect that the documents they read will have a relatively high level of visual appeal. Send someone a plain, unformatted memo and although they might not throw it out without a glance, they're likely to look down their noses at such a ragtag specimen. So, although you need to always ensure your content is up to snuff (accurate, grammatically correct, and so on), you also need to spend some time making sure that the content looks its best.

When you work with formatting in the Office for iPad apps, it helps to remember that there are only three main types of formatting and only two main methods for applying formatting.

Here are the three main types of formatting:

- **Font formatting**—This is also called *character formatting* and it refers to attributes applied to individual characters, including the font (or typeface), type size, text effects (such as bold, italic, and underline), and text color.

- **Paragraph formatting**—This refers to attributes applied to paragraphs as a whole, including indenting, alignment, line spacing, spacing before and after the paragraph, bullets, numbering, background shading, and borders.

- **Document formatting**—This refers to attributes applied to the document as a whole, including margins, headers, footers, columns, page orientation, paper size, columns, line numbers, and hyphenation.

Here are the two main methods for applying font and paragraph formatting in the Office for iPad apps:

- **Directly**—With this method, you select individual font and paragraph attributes. If you selected text beforehand, the app applies the formatting to the selection; otherwise, it applies the formatting to the current cursor position.

- **Styles**—A *style* is a predefined collection of formatting options. With this method, when you apply a style to text, the Office for iPad app applies all the style's formatting options at once. Also, if you change a formatting option within a style, all the text that uses that style is automatically updated with the new formatting. You'll find out more on this feature in the later section "Apply Styles."

Selecting Text

Before you can do anything with text in the Office for iPad apps—that is, before you can change the font, format paragraphs, apply styles, and so on—you need to tell the app which text you want to work with. You do that by selecting the text, which then appears on the screen with a blue background. This applies to text in Word, PowerPoint, and OneNote, as well as to text within an Excel cell. (To learn how to select multiple Excel cells, see "Select a Range" in Chapter 7, "Getting More Out of Excel Ranges.")

Select Text on a Touchscreen

The iPad is a touchscreen device, so you use gestures to select text.

1. Tap and hold the first word you want to include in the selection, and then release when the magnified version of the word appears.

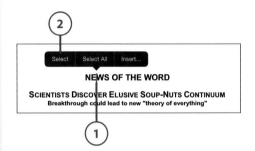

Selecting Text in Excel

Before you can select text in Excel, you must first open the cell for editing by double-tapping the cell. However, if you want to work with the entire cell, you can just tap the cell.

2. Tap Select. The app selects the word and displays the selection handles.

3. If you need to adjust where the selection begins, tap and drag the start selection handle to the left until the first character you want to include in the selection is highlighted.

4. If you need to adjust where the selection ends, tap and drag the end selection handle to the right until the last character you want to include in the selection is highlighted.

5. When you no longer require the text to be selected, tap somewhere else in the document.

Start selection handle

End selection handle

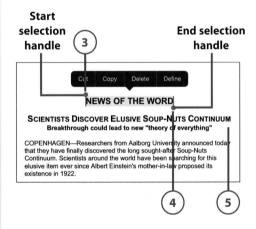

Touch Text Selection Tricks

In all the Office for iPad apps, you can select a single word by double-tapping that word. In Word, PowerPoint, and OneNote, you can select an entire paragraph by triple-tapping anywhere within that paragraph.

It's Not All Good

Selected Text Is Easily Deleted Text

When you select text—whether it's just a few characters, a word or two, or one or more paragraphs—the Office for iPad apps treat that selection as a single item. That's normally a good thing because it means that when you perform an operation such as applying formatting, the app applies the format to the entire selection. On the downside, it also means that you can easily delete the selection by mistake. If you have text selected when you press a character, the app immediately deletes the selected text and replaces it with that character! So exercise caution around a keyboard while you have text selected. If you do accidentally deleted the selected text, immediately tap Undo on the Ribbon.

Changing the Font

Windows and Mac OS X have turned many otherwise ordinary citizens into avid amateur typographers. Users at cocktail parties the world over are debating the relative merits of "serif" versus "sans serif" fonts, expounding the virtues of typefaces with names like Calibri and Helvetica, and throwing around font jargon terms such as ascender, feet, and points. (If many, or even all, of these terms are new to you, not to worry: I explain them all in this chapter.)

Okay, so most of us don't take fonts to that extreme. However, we certainly appreciate what they do to jazz up our reports, spreadsheets, and presentations. There's nothing like a well-chosen font to add just the right tone to a document and to make our work stand out from the herd.

I always like to describe fonts as the "architecture" of characters. When you examine a building, certain features and patterns help you identify the building's architectural style. A flying buttress, for example, is usually a telltale sign of a Gothic structure. Fonts, too, are distinguished by a unique set of characteristics. Specifically, four items define the architecture of any character: typeface, type size, type effects, and type color. I discuss all four characteristics in the sections that follow and show you how to apply them using the Office for iPad apps.

Understanding Typefaces

A typeface is a distinctive design that's common to any related set of letters, numbers, and symbols. This design gives each character a particular shape and thickness (or weight, as it's called in type circles) that's unique to the typeface and difficult to classify. However, four main categories serve to distinguish all typefaces:

- **Serif**—A serif (rhymes with *sheriff*) typeface contains fine cross strokes (called *feet*) at the extremities of each character. These subtle appendages give the typeface a traditional, classy look that's most often used for titles and headings. The Office for iPad apps come with several serif typefaces, including Cambria and Times New Roman.

- **Sans serif**—A sans serif typeface doesn't contain cross strokes on the extremities of characters. As a result, sans serif typefaces usually have a cleaner, more modern look that works best for regular text. The default Office for iPad typeface for document text, Calibri, is a sans serif typeface.

- **Fixed-width**—A fixed-width typeface—also called a *monospace* typeface—uses the same amount of space for each character, so skinny letters such as *i* and *l* take up as much space as wider letters such as *m* and *w*. Although this is admirably egalitarian, these fonts tend to look as if they were produced with a typewriter. (In other words, they're ugly.) Courier New is an example of a fixed-width typeface.

- **Decorative**—Decorative typefaces are usually special designs that are supposed to convey a particular effect. So, for example, if your document needs a fancy, handwritten effect, a font like Snell Roundhand is perfect.

Note, too, that the Office for iPad apps divide typefaces into two categories:

- **Office Compatible Fonts**—These are fonts that are supported by all current versions of Microsoft Office. If you use these fonts, you can be sure that your documents will look the same in any version of Office.

- **iOS Fonts**—These are the fonts that come with your iPad. (iOS is the name of the operating system used by the iPad.) These are fine if you'll be working only with a document on your iPad, but there's no guarantee the fonts will be supported on other computers or devices.

Set the Typeface

When setting the typeface, you can apply it either to existing text or to text that you're about to add to the document.

1. Select the text you want to format. Or if you want to format the next text you type, position the cursor where you want the text to appear.

2. Tap the Home tab.

3. Tap the Font list.

4. Tap the typeface you want to use. The app applies the typeface to the text.

Tap *i* to see other members of the font family

Change the Type Size

You can use type sizes to gain more control over the display of a document. For example, if you want to emphasize a title or heading, you can increase the type size. Similarly, if you want to fit more text into a particular area—such as a worksheet cell or a PowerPoint text box—you can decrease the type size.

1. Select the text you want to format. Or if you want to format the next text you type, position the cursor where you want the text to appear.

2. Tap the Home tab.

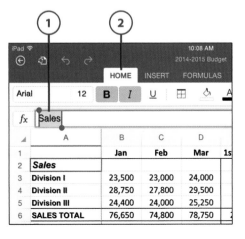

3. Tap the Font Size list.

4. Tap the type size you want to use. The Office for iPad app applies the type size to the text.

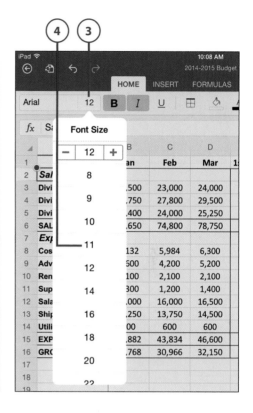

>>>Go Further

UNDERSTANDING TYPE SIZE

The *type size* measures the height of a font. The standard unit of measurement is the *point*, where there are 72 points in one inch. So, for example, the letters in a 24-point font are twice as tall as those in a 12-point font. Technically, type size is measured from the highest point of any letter with an *ascender*, which is the top part of a letter that extends above the letter body (such as the lowercase *f* and *h*), to the lowest point of a letter with a *descender*, which is the bottom part a letter that extends below the letter baseline (such as the lowercase *g* or *y*). (In case you're wondering, this book is laid out in a 10-point Myriad Pro font.)

Apply Type Effects

The *type effects* of a font refer to extra attributes added to the typeface, such as **bold** and *italic*. Other type effects (often called type styles) include <u>underline</u> and ~~strikethrough~~. You normally use these styles to highlight or add emphasis to text.

1. Select the text you want to format. Or if you want to format the next text you type, position the cursor where you want the text to appear.

2. Tap the Home tab.

3. Tap the icons to select the type effects you want to apply.

4. If you don't see the effect you want, tap the Font Formatting icon.

5. Tap the type effect you want to apply.

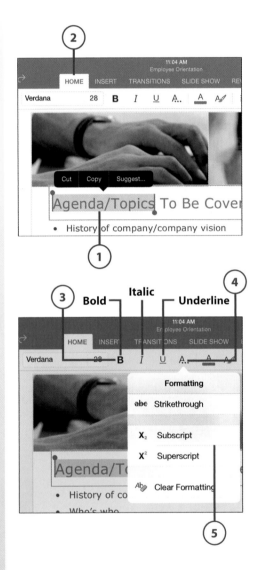

Set Text Colors

You can add some visual interest to your documents by changing the color of the document text. In most cases, you'll want to set the color of just the text. However, in Word and OneNote, you can also highlight sections of a document by applying a color to the text background. As with fonts, the colors you have available in Word, Excel, and PowerPoint depend on the theme applied to the document: Each theme comes with a palette of 60 colors. However, you can also choose a color from the app's palette of 10 standard colors.

1. Select the text you want to format. Or if you want to format the next text you type, position the cursor where you want the text to appear.

2. Tap the Home tab.

3. Tap the Font Color list.

4. Tap the tab for the color collection you want to use.

5. Tap the color you want to apply.

6. In Word and OneNote, you can also tap the Text Highlight Color list to apply a highlight to the text.

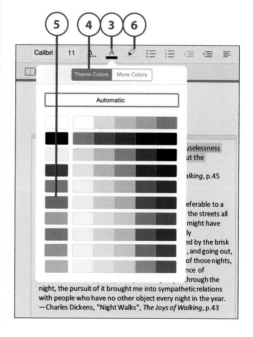

>>>*Go Further*
GETTING CREATIVE WITH A CUSTOM COLOR

The 60 colors that appear in the Theme Colors tab and the 10 standard colors that appear on the More Colors tab seem like a large palette, but you might not find the color that's just right for your needs. In that case, you take matters into your own hands and create the color you want. In the Font Color list, tap the More Colors tab, and then tap Custom Color to display the Custom Color dialog. In the larger palette on the left, tap the basic color you want to use. In the smaller palette on the right, tap and drag the bar to indicate how much gray you want in the custom color. Drag the bar up for a lighter hue (that is, less gray), or drag the bar down for a darker hue (more gray).

Formatting Paragraphs

The Word, PowerPoint, and OneNote apps are simple programs in the sense that it's easy to get started with them: You just create a new document or open an existing document and then start typing. Of course, not all documents consist of basic text. For example, you might require a bulleted or numbered list, or you might need to adjust the indentation or alignment of a paragraph. This section shows you how to perform these tasks in the Word, PowerPoint, and OneNote apps.

Align Paragraphs

You can make a document easier to read by aligning its text horizontally. You can align the text with the left margin (this is the default alignment), with the right margin, or with the center of the document. In Word, you can also justify a paragraph's text, which means the text gets aligned with both the left and right margins.

1. Tap inside the paragraph or cell you want to align. If you want to align multiple items, select some or all the text in each of the paragraphs or select each cell.

2. Tap the Home tab.

3. Tap Alignment.

4. Tap the alignment you want to apply.

Applying Alignment

You can apply these alignments to one or more paragraphs in a Word document, to one or more cells in an Excel worksheet, to text in a PowerPoint slide, or to paragraphs in a OneNote page.

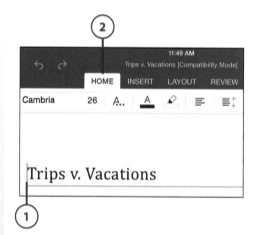

Set the Line Spacing

You can improve the look of your document by adjusting the line spacing, which determines the amount of space between each line in a paragraph. For example, double spacing leaves twice as much space between the lines as the standard single spacing. Increasing the spaces creates more white space in the document, which can make the document easier to read.

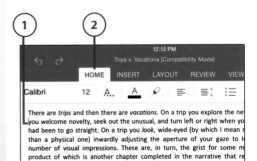

1. Tap inside the paragraph you want to format. If you want to set the spacing for multiple paragraphs, select some or all the text in each of the paragraphs.

2. Tap the Home tab.

3. Tap Line Spacing.

4. Tap the line spacing value that you want to apply.

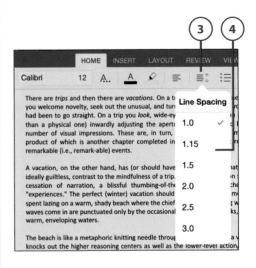

Applying Line Spacing

You can adjust line spacing to one or more paragraphs in a Word document. However, the line spacing feature is not available in the Excel, PowerPoint, and OneNote apps.

Build a Bulleted List

You can make a list of items more prominent and more readable by formatting those items as a bulleted list. When you do, the app formats the items slightly indented from the regular text, with a small character—called the bullet, which is usually a black dot—in front of each item.

You can either create a bulleted list from scratch or convert an existing list of items to a bulleted list. You also have a choice of several different bullet characters.

1. If you want to convert existing text to a bulleted list, select the text.

Converting Text to a Bulleted List

If you're selecting text to convert to a bulleted list, the text must be a series of items, of any length, each in its own paragraph.

2. Tap the Home tab.

3. Tap Bullets.

4. Tap the bullet style you want to use. If you selected your text in advance, the app converts the text to a bulleted list.

5. If you selected text in advance, tap at the end of the last item. The insertion point moves to the end of the item.

6. Press Return. The app creates a new item in the bulleted list.

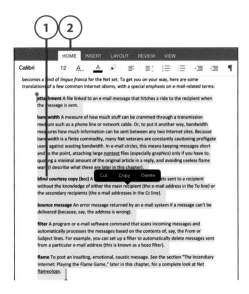

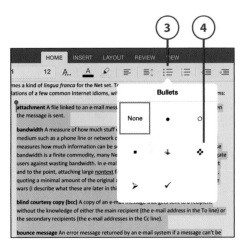

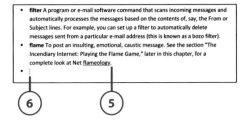

7. Type the text for the new list item.

8. Repeat steps 6 and 7 until you complete the bulleted list.

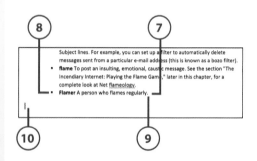

Creating Subbullets

If you want to shift a list item so that it's a subbullet of the item above it, tap at the beginning of the item and then tap Increase Indent. To return the item to its previous level, tap Decrease Indent.

9. Tap at the end of the last item.

10. Press Return twice. The app ends the bulleted list.

Create a Numbered List

You can make a set of steps or an ordered list more readable and easier to follow by formatting those items as a numbered list. When you do, the app formats the items slightly indented from the regular text, with a number in front of each item. The numbers increase sequentially, usually from 1 to the total number of items in the list.

You can either create a numbered list from scratch or convert an existing list of items to a numbered list. You also have a choice of several different numbering characters.

1. If you want to convert existing text to a numbered list, select the text.

2. Tap the Home tab.

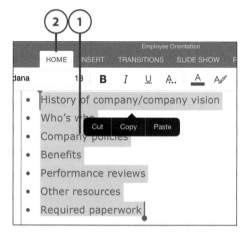

Converting Text to a Numbered List

If you're selecting text to convert to a numbered list, the text must be a series of items, of any length, each in its own paragraph.

3. Tap Numbering.

4. Tap the number format you want to use. If you selected your text in advance, the app converts the text to a numbered list.

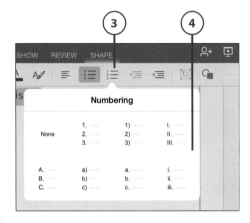

Number Formats

The number formats are only available in the Word and PowerPoint apps. In OneNote, when you tap Numbering, the app applies a default numbered list format.

5. If you selected the text in advance, tap at the end of the last item. The insertion point moves to the end of the item.

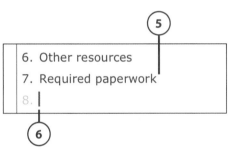

6. Press Return. The app creates a new item in the numbered list.

7. Type the text for the new list item.

8. Repeat steps 6 and 7 until you complete the numbered list.

9. Tap at the end of the last item.

10. Press Return twice. The app ends the numbered list. (If you still see the next number in PowerPoint, tap Backspace to delete it.)

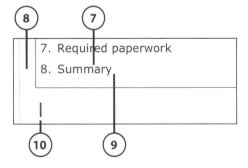

Set the Indentation

You can set a paragraph off from the rest of the text by indenting the paragraph. For example, if a document includes a lengthy quotation, you can indent the quotation to make it stand out. In the Word, PowerPoint, and OneNote apps, you can indent a paragraph from the left.

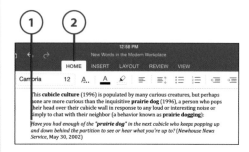

1. Tap inside the paragraph you want to indent. If you want to indent multiple paragraphs, select some or all the text in each of the paragraphs.

2. Tap the Home tab.

3. Tap Increase Indent. The app shifts the entire paragraph away from the left margin.

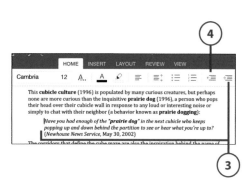

4. Repeat step 3 until the paragraph is indented the amount you want. If you indent a paragraph too much, you can shift the text back toward the left margin by tapping Decrease Indent.

Working with Formatting

Working with text and paragraph formatting can be time-consuming and labor-intensive. It's almost always worth the extra effort to make your Office documents look their best, but that doesn't mean you should waste time performing your formatting chores. The Office for iPad apps offer a few handy features that can help reduce the amount of time and effort you expend on your formatting, and the rest of this chapter covers these useful tools.

Apply Styles

You can save time and effort when formatting your documents by taking advantage of the predefined styles that are available in the Office for iPad apps. A style is a collection of formatting options, usually including some or all the following: typeface, type size, text color, text effects, and paragraph alignment. When you apply a style to some text, the app applies all the style's formatting at once.

1. Select the text you want to format.

2. Tap the Home tab.

3. Tap Styles.

4. Tap the style you want to use. The Office app applies the style's formatting to the text.

Applying Styles by App

The Styles command is available in Word, PowerPoint, and OneNote. In Excel, tap Cell Styles, instead.

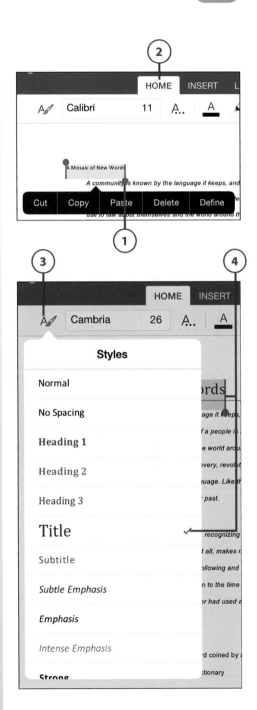

Apply Text Effects

The Office styles apply standard font formatting such as bold, font size, and font color. If you're looking for something with a bit more pizzazz, you can format your words with a text effect, which is a preset style that applies more advanced formatting such as reflections, textures, and 3-D effects.

1. Select the text you want to format.

2. Tap the Home tab.

3. Tap Formatting.

4. Tap Text Effects.

5. Tap a text effect. Word applies the effect to the selected text.

Text Effects Are Word-Only

The Text Effects feature is only available in the Word app.

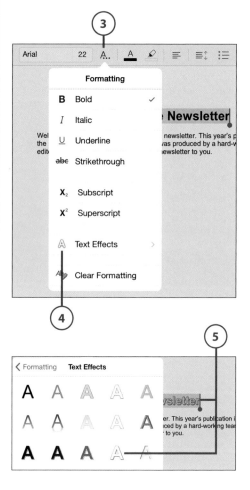

Clear Formatting

If you apply a number of font formats, paragraph options, or styles to some text, you might decide later that you no longer want any of that formatting. Although it's possible to turn off or remove each of the formatting options individually, the Word and PowerPoint apps offer a much easier method: the Clear Formatting command. Tapping this command removes all formatting from the selected text, so this method is much easier than trying to clear the formatting options one by one.

1. Select the text you want to clear.

2. Tap the Home tab.

3. Tap Formatting.

4. Tap Clear Formatting. The Office app clears all formatting from the text.

Apply picture styles   Add a shadow   Display a reflection   Rotate a graphic

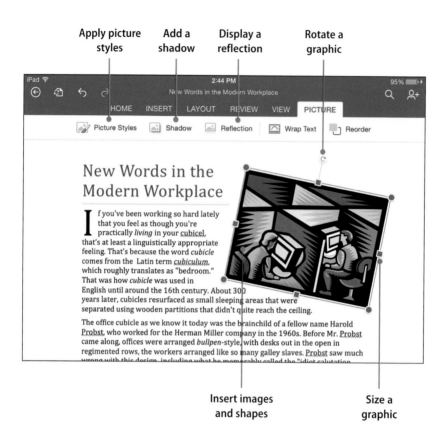

Insert images and shapes   Size a graphic

In this chapter, you learn various techniques for drawing, inserting, and working with graphics such as lines, shapes, and photos.

→ Inserting photos
→ Drawing lines, rectangles, and circles
→ Selecting one or more graphics
→ Sizing, moving, and rotating graphics
→ Applying styles and effects to graphics

3

Working with Office for iPad Graphics

When most people think about using the Office for iPad apps, they generally think about text, whether it's writing sentences and paragraphs in Word, adding formulas and labels in Excel, creating slide titles and bullets in PowerPoint, and so on. It is certainly true that most of the work people do in Office for iPad—from writing papers to generating purchase orders to creating presentations—is and should remain text-based.

However, if you think only text when you think of Office, you're missing out on a whole other dimension. All the Office for iPad apps have a small but useful collection of graphics tools that you can take advantage of to improve the clarity of your work or just to add a bit of pizzazz to liven up an otherwise drab document.

Even better, these graphics tools work the same across apps, so when you learn how to use them, you can apply your knowledge to any program. This chapter shows you how to create, edit, and enhance graphics in the Office for iPad apps.

Inserting Images

To spruce up your Office for iPad documents, the apps come with commands that you can use to insert several types of images:

- **Picture**—You can enhance the visual appeal and strengthen the message of a document by adding a picture to the file. The Office for iPad apps can work with the most popular picture formats, including BMP, JPEG, TIFF, PNG, and GIF. This means that you can insert almost any photo that you have stored on your iPad.

- **Shape**—This is an object such as a line or rectangle that you draw within your document. You can use shapes to point out key features in a document, enclose text, create flowcharts, and enhance the look of a document. Office for iPad offers a number of shape types, including the following:

  - **Lines**—Straight lines, squiggles, free-form polygons, arrows, connectors, and curves

  - **Rectangles**—Rectangles, rounded rectangles, and more

  - **Basic Shapes**—Triangles, circles, boxes, cylinders, hearts, and many more

  - **Block Arrows**—Two-dimensional arrows of various configurations

  - **Equation Shapes**—Two-dimensional images for the basic arithmetic symbols, such as plus (+) and equals (=)

  - **Flowchart**—The standard shapes used for creating flowcharts

  - **Stars and Banners**—Stars, starbursts, scrolls, and more

  - **Callouts**—Boxes and lines for creating callouts to document features

- **Text box**—The graphics you add to your documents will usually consist of images, but sometimes you'll need to augment those images with some text. For example, you might want to add a title and subtitle or insert a label.

Insert a Picture

If you have a photo or other image on your iPad that you think would add just the right touch, you can insert it into your document.

1. Tap where you want the picture to appear.

2. Tap the Insert tab.

3. Tap the Pictures icon to open the Photos dialog.

4. Tap the album that contains the picture you want to insert.

5. Tap the picture.

6. If you're using OneNote, tap the Crop icon if you want to use only part of the picture.

Cropping a Picture

To crop the picture in OneNote, tap the Crop icon to display a cropping grid, drag the corners of the grid to specify the portion of the picture you want to keep, and then tap OK (the check mark).

---

7. Tap the check mark. The app inserts the picture into the document.

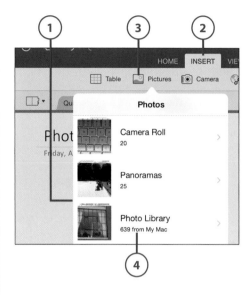

>>>Go Further
TAKING A PHOTO IN ONENOTE

You can save a moment for posterity by taking a picture with one of the iPad's cameras and storing the photo in a OneNote notebook. To do this, open OneNote, open the notebook you want to use, display the page where you want the photo stored, and then tap inside the page. Tap Insert and then tap Camera to open the Camera app. Tap Photo if you're taking a regular photo; tap Whiteboard if you're taking a picture of whiteboard text; or tap Document if you're shooting document text. Tap the purple Shutter button to take the picture. Tap the check mark in the lower-right corner of the screen. If you see a message telling you that OneNote would like to access your photos, tap OK.

Insert a Line

You can use lines to point out important document information, create
a free-form drawing, or as part of
a more complex graphic such as
a company logo. You can insert a
straight line, which can have an
arrowhead at one or both ends, or
a connector, a multisegment line or
curve normally used to connect two
other objects.

1. Tap the Insert tab.

2. Tap Shapes.

3. Tap the shape you want from
   the Lines section. The app adds a
   default shape to the document.

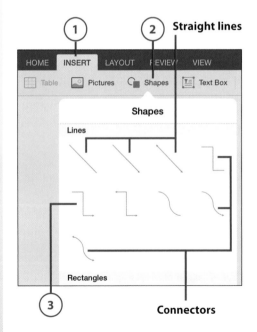

4. Tap and drag the ends of the line or curve to set the length and orientation.

5. If you inserted a connector, tap and drag the yellow handle to set the position of the middle segment of a line connector, or the extent of the curve in a curve connector.

Insert Any Other Shape

You can use the other shapes either on their own—for example, to point out features with callouts or block arrows or to enhance text with stars or banners—or as part of a more complex graphic.

1. Tap the Insert tab.

2. Tap Shapes.

3. Tap the shape you want. The app adds a default shape to the document.

4. Tap and drag the shape's sizing handles until the shape has the size and form you want and then release.

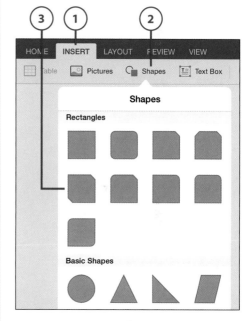

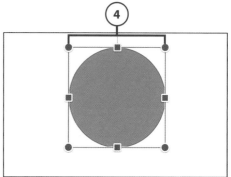

Insert a Text Box

The graphics you add to your documents will usually consist of images, but sometimes you'll need to augment those images with text. For example, you might want to add a title and subtitle or insert a label. If a WordArt image seems like overkill for this, then a better alternative is to draw a text box and type your text within that box.

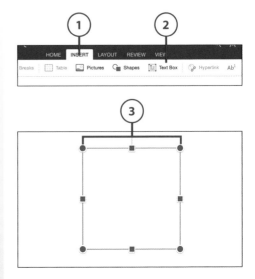

1. Tap the Insert tab.

2. Tap Text Box. The app adds a default shape to the document.

3. Tap and drag the text box sizing handles until the box has the size and form you want and then release.

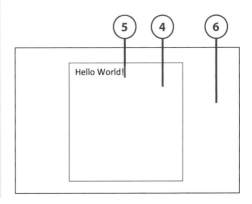

4. Double-tap inside the text box.

5. Type your text.

6. When you're done, tap outside the text box.

Working with Graphics

Inserting a line, shape, picture, or other graphic object is usually only one-half the battle. To complete your work with the graphic, you usually need to spend a bit of time formatting and editing the object to get it just right. This may include some or all the following: sizing the graphic; rotating it; moving it; and determining whether a graphic appears on top of or behind any other graphics in your document. This section provides you with the details of these and other techniques for working with graphics.

Size a Graphic

If a graphic is too large or too small for your needs, or if the object's shape is not what you want, you can size the image to change its dimensions or its shape. You might want to size a graphic so that it fits within an open document area.

1. Tap the graphic you want to size.

2. To adjust the width of the graphic, drag the left or right handle.

3. To adjust the height of the graphic, drag the top or bottom handle.

4. To adjust the width and height at the same time, drag a corner handle.

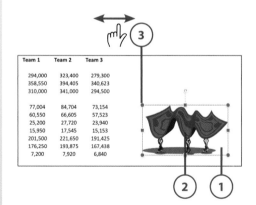

Sizing handles appear around the edges of a selected object

Move a Graphic

To ensure that a graphic is ideally placed within a document, you can move the graphic to a new location. For example, you might want to move a graphic so that it does not cover existing document text.

1. Tap the graphic you want to move.

2. Place a finger in the middle of the object. Make sure you don't place your finger over any of the object's sizing handles.

3. Drag the object to the position you want.

Rotate a Graphic

Most graphic objects get inserted into a document without any rotation: Horizontal borders appear horizontal, and vertical borders appear vertical. A nonrotated image is probably what you will want most of the time, but for some occasions an image tilted at a jaunty angle is just the right touch for a document. Many objects come with a rotation handle that you can use to rotate the object clockwise or counterclockwise.

1. Tap the graphic you want to rotate.

2. Use a finger to drag the rotation handle. Drag the handle clockwise to rotate the graphic clockwise; drag the handle counterclockwise to rotate the graphic counterclockwise.

Rotation handle 1

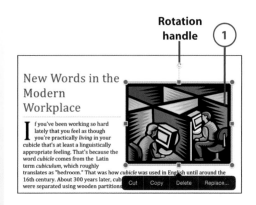

Reorder Graphics

If a document has multiple images that overlap each other, you've probably noticed that some images appear "on top" of others. This is determined by the stacking order, and usually images added later are added "above" existing images. You can change this either by sending an image toward the back of the stack (so it appears beneath some or all the other images) or by bringing an image toward the front of the stack (so that it appears on top of some or all the other images).

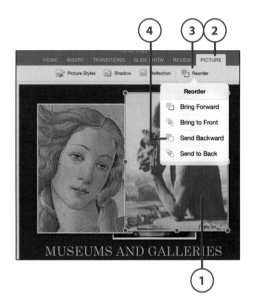

1. Tap the graphic you want to reorder.

2. Tap the Picture tab.

3. Tap Reorder.

4. To send the image toward the back of the stack, tap Send Backward; to bring the image toward the front of the stack, tap Bring Forward.

Reordering All the Way Backward or Forward

If you want the graphic to end up behind every other graphic in the document, tap Send to Back to place it at the back of the stack. If you want the graphic to end up in front of every other graphic in the document, tap Bring to Front to place it at the front of the stack.

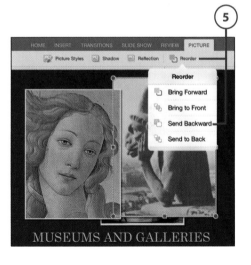

5. Repeat Steps 3 and 4 until the graphic is in the stack position you want.

Formatting Graphics

When your shape or picture is sized, positioned, rotated, and ordered, you're ready to make it look good by formatting the graphic. The Office for iPad apps come with a number of image formatting tools that enables you to apply styles, add shadows and reflections, change fills and lines, and format graphic text. The rest of this chapter provides you with the details of these and other techniques that you can use to format graphic objects.

Apply a Picture Style

You can enhance your pictures by formatting the images. For example, the Office for iPad apps offer more than two dozen picture styles, which are predefined formats that apply various combinations of shadows, reflections, borders, and layouts.

1. Tap the picture you want to format.

2. Tap the Picture tab.

3. Tap Picture Styles. The Picture Styles gallery appears.

4. Tap the picture style you want to use. The app applies the style to the picture.

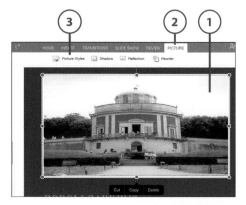

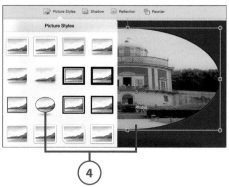

It's Not All Good

Reverting to the Original

After playing around with a graphic for a while, you might end up with a bit of a mess. If you don't like the formatting that you've applied to a graphic, you might prefer to return the picture to its original look and start over. If you haven't performed any other tasks since applying the formatting, tap Undo until the app has removed the formatting.

Add a Picture Shadow

You can add an interesting lighting effect to a document by applying a shadow effect to the document graphics. You can make a picture stand out from the document by applying an outer shadow or perspective shadow; and you can make a picture look set into the document by applying an inner shadow.

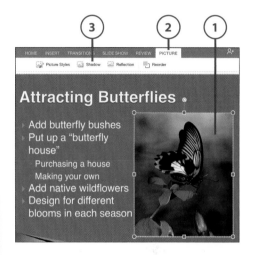

1. Tap the picture you want to format.

2. Tap the Picture tab.

3. Tap Shadow. The Shadow gallery appears.

4. Tap the shadow effect you want to apply. The app applies the shadow to the picture.

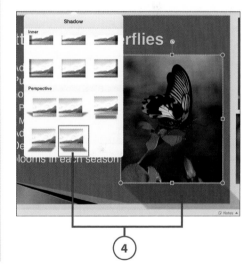

It's Not All Good

Reverting to the Original

If you later decide that the shadow effect isn't right for your document, you can remove it. If you haven't performed any other tasks since applying the shadow, tap Undo to remove it. Otherwise, tap the picture, tap the Picture tab, tap Shadow, and then tap No Shadow.

Enhance a Picture with a Reflection

A simple but attention-grabbing look for a picture is a reflection, which makes it appears as though the picture is resting on a shiny surface. The Office for iPad apps offer several reflection styles that vary the intensity and length of the reflection.

1. Tap the picture you want to format.

2. Tap the Picture tab.

3. Tap Reflection. The Reflection gallery appears.

4. Tap the reflection type you want to apply. The app applies the reflection to the picture.

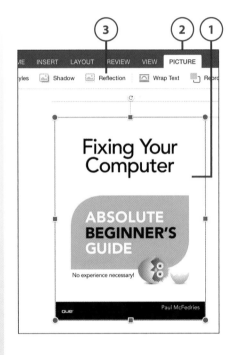

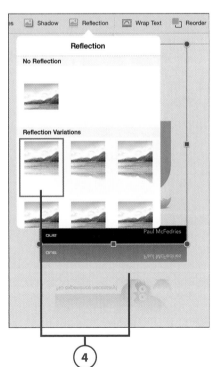

Apply a Shape Style

You can enhance your shapes by applying one of Office for iPad's apps that offer more than 40 shape styles, which are predefined formats that apply various combinations of colors, gradients, and 3-D effects.

1. Tap the shape you want to format.

2. Tap the Shape tab.

3. Tap Shape Styles. The Shape Styles gallery appears.

4. Tap the shape style you want to use. The app applies the style to the shape.

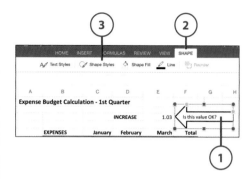

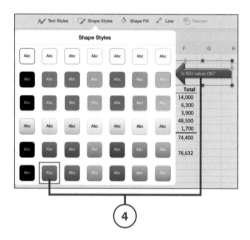

Format the Shape Line and Fill

Each shape has two characteristics that you can customize: the line, which is the outline of the shape, and the fill, which is the interior of the shape (assuming it has one; a line, for example, doesn't have a fill). In both cases, you can choose from a palette of 60 colors associated with the document's theme, as well as the app's palette of 10 standard colors.

1. Tap the shape you want to format.

2. Tap the Shape tab.

3. Tap Line. The Line gallery appears.

4. Tap the tab for the color collection you want to use.

5. Tap the color you want to apply. The app applies the color to the shape's line.

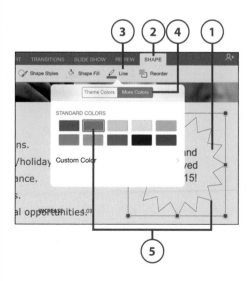

6. Tap Shape Fill. The Shape Fill gallery appears.

7. Tap the tab for the color collection you want to use.

8. Tap the color you want to apply. The app applies the color to the shape's fill.

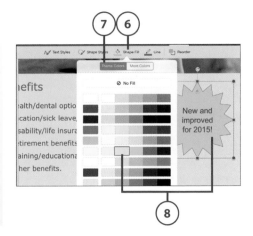

>>>Go Further

GETTING CREATIVE WITH A CUSTOM COLOR

Despite the 60 colors that appear on the Theme Colors tab and the 10 standard colors that appear on the More Colors tab, you might not find the exact color you need. To create a custom color, open the Line or Shape Fill gallery, tap the More Colors tab, and then tap Custom Color to display the Custom Color dialog. In the larger palette on the left, tap the basic color you want to use. In the smaller palette on the right, tap and drag the bar to indicate how much gray you want in the custom color. Drag the bar up for a lighter hue (that is, less gray), or drag the bar down for a darker hue (more gray).

Set the Text Style for a Shape or Text Box

If you've added text to a shape or to a text box, you can format that text using the standard font commands on the Home tab. However, Office for iPad also offers the Text Styles gallery, which comes with 20 predefined formats that can give your graphic text little extra oomph.

1. Tap the shape or text box you want to format.

2. Tap the Shape tab.

3. Tap Text Styles. The Text Styles gallery appears.

4. Tap the style you want to apply. The app applies the style to the shape or text box text.

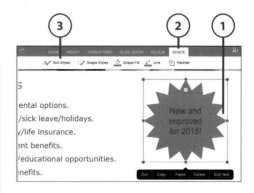

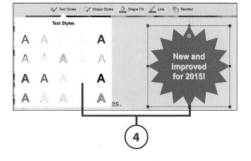

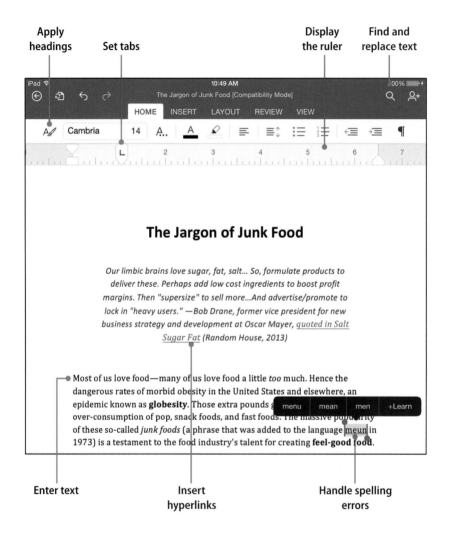

Apply headings

Set tabs

Display the ruler

Find and replace text

iPad 📶   10:49 AM   00% 🔋

The Jargon of Junk Food [Compatibility Mode]

HOME   INSERT   LAYOUT   REVIEW   VIEW

Cambria   14

The Jargon of Junk Food

Our limbic brains love sugar, fat, salt... So, formulate products to deliver these. Perhaps add low cost ingredients to boost profit margins. Then "supersize" to sell more...And advertise/promote to lock in "heavy users." —Bob Drane, former vice president for new business strategy and development at Oscar Mayer, quoted in Salt Sugar Fat (Random House, 2013)

Most of us love food—many of us love food a little *too* much. Hence the dangerous rates of morbid obesity in the United States and elsewhere, an epidemic known as **globesity**. Those extra pounds g— — — over-consumption of pop, snack foods, and fast foods. The massive popularity of these so-called *junk foods* (a phrase that was added to the language meun in 1973) is a testament to the food industry's talent for creating **feel-good food**.

menu   mean   men   +Learn

Enter text

Insert hyperlinks

Handle spelling errors

In this chapter, you learn about working with text in Word, including entering and editing text, inserting symbols, tabs, and hyperlinks, finding text, and handling spelling mistakes.

→ Entering and editing Word text

→ Adding tabs and headings

→ Finding and replacing document text

→ Handling spelling errors

→ Adding hyperlinks

Working with Text in Word

All the Office for iPad apps require at least some written input. From worksheet titles and labels in Excel to slide headings and bullets in PowerPoint to page snippets and lists in OneNote, you always work with text in one form or another when you work with Office for iPad. However, when you have some serious writing to do, the Office for iPad tool of choice is, of course, Word with its word processing pedigree. Whether you're composing your next blog post or firing off a memo to the troops, Word can handle almost any text task you throw at it.

Word is loaded with useful and powerful features that can help you not only create beautiful documents, but also create those documents in record time. The next few chapters are designed to introduce you to these features and other techniques for getting the most out of Word on the iPad. This chapter gets you off to a good start by examining a number of handy and powerful techniques for entering and editing text in Word.

Learning Text Basics

Fritterware refers to software programs that contain so many bells and whistles that you can't help but fritter away huge amounts of time trying out different options and features. Fortunately, that is not a term that applies to Word for iPad. This is a streamlined, elegant version of Word that offers just the tools you need, not every tool there is. (That's reserved for the desktop version of Word!)

Word for iPad is ideally suited for entering text, which means you can become immediately more productive if you learn a few techniques for making text entry easier and faster.

Enter and Edit Text

Although you can attach a physical keyboard, you'll most likely use your iPad's onscreen keyboard to enter and edit text in Word (and, indeed, in all the Office for iPad apps).

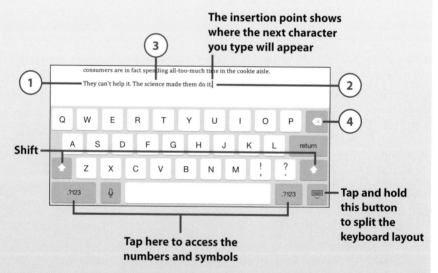

The insertion point shows where the next character you type will appear

Tap and hold this button to split the keyboard layout

Tap here to access the numbers and symbols

1. Tap at the spot where you want to start entering text. If the document already contains text, tap at the spot where you want your next typing to appear.

2. Type your text.

3. To edit text, tap at the spot where you want to make your changes.

4. Tap Backspace to delete the character to the left of the insertion point.

>>>Go Further
SPLITTING THE KEYBOARD

If you plan on doing a lot of typing using the iPad's onscreen keyboard, consider splitting the keyboard, which divides the keyboard layout in two and displays one-half by the left edge of the screen and the other half by the right edge. This layout makes typing easier and faster when you're holding the iPad because all the keys are within reach of your thumbs.

To split the keyboard, tap and hold the button in the lower-right corner of the keyboard until a menu of commands appears. Then slide your finger up into the menu and release when the Split common is highlighted. You can then tap and drag the same button up or down to position the keyboard.

To return to the regular layout, tap and hold the same button; then slide your finger to the Dock and Merge command.

Entering Text with Shortcuts

Most of us have phrases, sentences, even multiple paragraphs that we add to our documents regularly. Such frequently used bits of text are called boilerplate, and having to type them constantly can be both tedious and time-wasting. To reduce the drudgery of boilerplate, you can set up shortcuts to store the boilerplate phrases and then recall each with a few keystrokes.

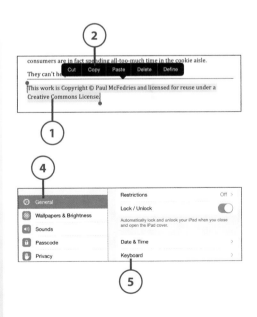

1. If you have an example of the boilerplate text, select it.

2. Tap Copy.

3. Open the Settings app.

4. Tap General.

5. Tap Keyboard.

6. Tap Add New Shortcut.

7. Tap inside the Phrase text box.

8. If you copied the boilerplate text, tap Paste. Otherwise, type your boilerplate text.

9. In the Shortcut text box, type a short abbreviation or code.

10. Tap Save.

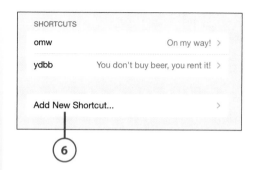

Using Your Shortcut

To insert a boilerplate phrase in your Word document, type your shortcut text; then press the spacebar or Return.

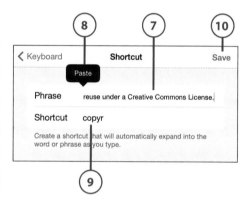

Insert Symbols

Word for iPad doesn't come with a command for inserting symbols, but the iPad keyboard does come with a few built-in symbols that you can reveal by tapping and holding a key. For example, if you tap and hold the $ key, you see several extra symbols, including signs for the British pound (£), cents (¢), the euro (€), and the Japanese yen (¥). Slide your finger up to the symbol you want and then release to insert it.

A few other symbols are available via Word's AutoCorrect, which means you just need to type the three or four original characters and Word converts them to the symbol automatically. The following table lists Word's predefined AutoCorrect entries for symbols.

Type	To Insert	Description
(c)	©	Copyright symbol
(r)	®	Registered trademark symbol
(tm)	™	Trademark symbol
...	...	Ellipsis

Display the Ruler

If you want to see or work with a paragraph's indents, hanging indents, or tabs, you need to display Word's ruler, which is hidden by default.

1. Tap the View tab.

2. Tap the Ruler switch to On.

The ruler

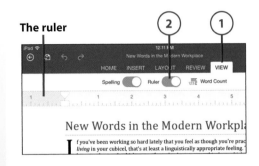

Set Tabs

Documents look much better if they're properly indented and if their various parts line up nicely. The best way to do this is to use tabs instead of spaces whenever you need to create some room in a line because a single space can take up different amounts of room, depending on the font and size of the characters you're using. So your document can end up looking quite ragged if you try to use spaces to indent your text. Tabs, on the other hand, are fastidiously precise: When you insert a tab, the insertion point moves ahead exactly to the next tab stop, no more, no less.

1. Select the paragraphs you want to format.

2. Tap the ruler at the position where you want the tab to appear. Word adds a tab indicator to that spot.

Tab indicator

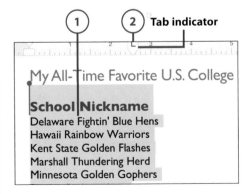

Move a Tab

If the tab isn't exactly where you want it, tap and drag the tab left or right along the ruler to set the correct position.

3. To add a tab, first tap and hold where you want the tab to appear.

4. Tap Insert.

5. Tap Tab. Word inserts the tab.

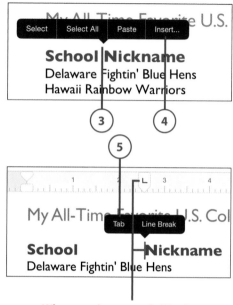

Delete a Tab

If you no longer need a tab, you should delete it from the ruler. To do that, tap and drag the tab indicator down until it's off the ruler, and then release.

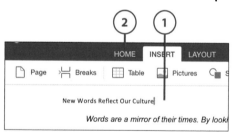

When you insert a tab, Word moves the text ahead to the next tab stop

Enter Headings

Headings are special paragraphs that serve as titles for different sections of a document. You specify headings in Word by applying a heading style, where the Heading 1 style is for the main sections of the document, Heading 2 is for the subsections, and Heading 3 is for the sub-subsections.

1. Tap inside the paragraph you want to turn into a heading.

2. Tap the Home tab.

3. Tap the Styles icon.

4. Tap the heading style you want to apply.

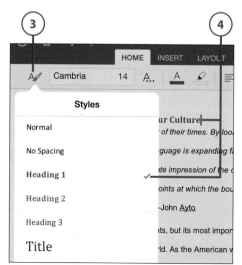

>>>*Go Further*

GETTING MORE HEADING STYLES

By default, Word for iPad supports only the styles Heading 1, Heading 2, and in some templates, Heading 3. That's all you'll need most of the time, but some documents might require a deeper hierarchy that includes Heading 4, Heading 5, and so on. You can't get that extended hierarchy in Word for iPad, but it's available in the desktop version of Word, which supports headings styles up to Heading 9. The good news is that if you add any of these lower-in-the-hierarchy headings to your document using desktop Word and then open that document in Word for iPad, all those heading styles become available.

Finding and Replacing Text

We're living in a world in which the dream of "information at your fingertips" is fast becoming a reality. Thanks to wireless network connections and portable web surfing devices such as your iPad, we can call up just about any tidbit of information we need with only a minimum of fuss.

This is fine for "Googleable" online info, but some of your most useful data probably resides within your own documents. Locating information in a small document is not usually a problem, but it's when your Word documents grow to tens of pages that locating the text you want becomes a real needle-in-a-haystack exercise. You can make it much easier to locate text in large documents by using Word's Find feature. Word also comes with a powerful Replace feature that enables you to quickly and easily replace multiple instances of a word or phrase with something else.

Find Text

Word's Find feature not only locates a word or phrase, but also offers options for matching uppercase and lowercase letters, and finding whole words only.

1. Tap the Find icon, which looks like a magnifying glass.

2. To specify search options, tap the Options icon.

3. Tap the Options icon to hide the Options dialog.

4. Use the text box to type the text you're looking for. Word selects the next instance of the text.

5. Tap the Next or Previous arrow to select more instances of the search text. Repeat as needed to find the instance of the text that you're looking for.

6. When you're done, tap anywhere in the document to hide the Find bar.

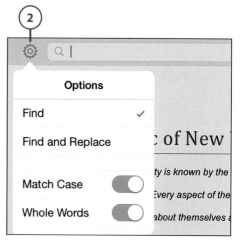

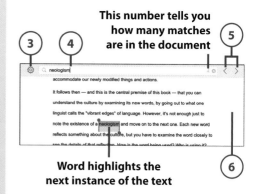

This number tells you how many matches are in the document

Word highlights the next instance of the text

>>>*Go Further*

SETTING FIND OPTIONS

You can use the switches in the Options dialog to refine your document searches. Tap the Match Case switch to On to find only those instances that match the uppercase and lowercase letters you specify in the Find What text box. For example, if you type **Bob** as the search text, Find will match *Bob* but not *bob* or *BOB*.

Tap the Whole Words switch to On to find only those instances of the search text that are entire words, not just partial words. For example, if you type **pen** as the search text, Find will match only the word *pen*, not words that contain pen, such as *expenses* and *pencil*.

Replace Text

If you have a number of instances of a word or phrase that require the same edit, performing each edit manually is too time-consuming. A much better method is to let Word's Replace feature handle some or all the edits for you.

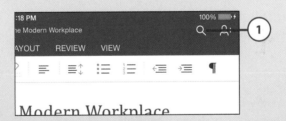

1. Tap the Find icon.

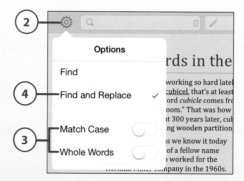

2. Tap the Options icon.

3. Specify your search options, if required.

4. Tap Find and Replace.

This number tells you how many matches are in the document

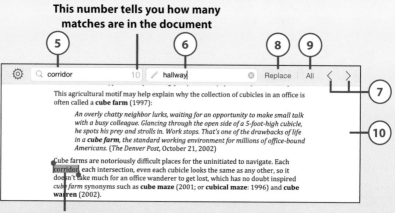

Word highlights the next instance of the text

5. Type the text you want to replace in the first text box. Word highlights the next instance of the Find What text.

6. Type the text you want to use as the replacement in the second text box.

7. Tap the Next or Previous arrow until the instance of the text that you want replaced is selected.

8. Tap Replace. Word makes the replacement and then selects the next instance.

9. Repeat steps 7 and 8 until you have changed all the instances you want replaced. Alternatively, you can tap All to replace every instance of the text in the document.

10. When you're done, tap anywhere in the document to hide the Find and Replace bar.

It's Not All Good

Replace All with Caution

The All command is the quickest and easiest way to make your replacements, but it's dangerous because you don't see every replacement that Word makes. This is particularly true if you use search options such as Match Case. Unless you're absolutely certain that you want to replace every instance in your document, use the Replace command instead of the All command.

Proofing Text

The word proofing is short for proofreading, and it refers to inspecting a body of writing for errors or inaccuracies. No matter what kind of writing you do, always proof your work before allowing other people to read it. One of the easiest ways to lose face in the working world or to lose marks in the academic world is to hand in a piece of writing that contains spelling mistakes. No matter how professionally organized and formatted your document appears, a simple spelling error will stick out and take your reader's mind off your message. However, mistakes do happen, especially if your document is a large one. To help you catch these errors, the iPad offers two features: Auto-Correction and Check Spelling.

As you type in Word (or any other app), iOS operates in the background and examines your text for errors. When you type a word-separating character (that is, you press the spacebar or Return or type a period, semicolon, comma, or colon), iOS compares the previous word with its internal dictionary. If it can't find the word in the dictionary, one of two things happens:

- If the error is a common one, Auto-Correction replaces the word with the correct one. For example, if you type **teh**, Auto-Correction replaces it with *the*.

- If a fix for the error can't be found, or if multiple fixes are available, Check Spelling signals the error by placing a wavy red line under the word. In this case, you need to handle the error yourself.

Handle Spelling Errors

If you have a word flagged as an error, you can handle it by applying one of Check Spellings suggested replacements, or by telling Check Spelling that the word is legitimate so that it doesn't flag the word again in the future.

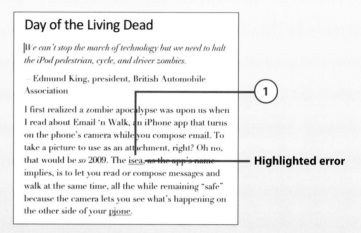

1. Tap a word that has been flagged as an error.

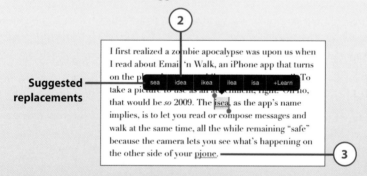

2. Tap one of the suggested corrections to the replace the existing word with the correction.

3. Repeat steps 1 and 2 until you have corrected all the spelling errors in your document.

Adding Correct Words to the Dictionary

Words such as proper names and technical terms are flagged by the spell checker because they don't appear in its dictionary of acceptable words. If the spell checker keeps flagging a correct word that you use frequently, you can add the word to its dictionary and thus avoid it getting flagged again. Tap the word and then tap Learn.

Adding Hyperlinks

A hyperlink is a special section of text that, when tapped, opens a website, and we're most familiar with them on web pages. Although web-based hyperlinks have been around for a long time now, it still seems slightly radical that you can insert a hyperlink in a Word document. This useful feature lets you create "active" documents that enable the reader to tap text to open the linked website in Safari.

Insert a Hyperlink

To insert a hyperlink in a Word document, you need to know the web address of the remote site or page. This is most easily accomplished by copying the address from Safari.

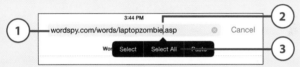

1. In Safari, tap the address box.
2. Tap and hold the address.
3. Tap Select All.

4. Tap Copy.

5. In Word, select the text you want to use as the hyperlink.
6. Tap the Insert tab.
7. Tap Hyperlink.

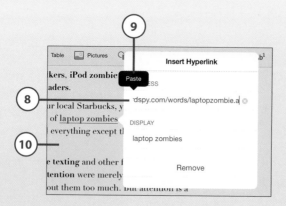

8. Tap inside the Address text box.

9. Tap Paste. Word pastes the address and creates the hyperlink.

10. Tap outside the Insert Hyperlink dialog to close it.

Removing a Hyperlink

If you no longer require a hyperlink in your Word document, you can remove it. To do this, tap the hyperlink, tap Edit, and then tap Remove.

Change
the page
orientation

Change the
paper size

Set the
margins

Add a header
and footer

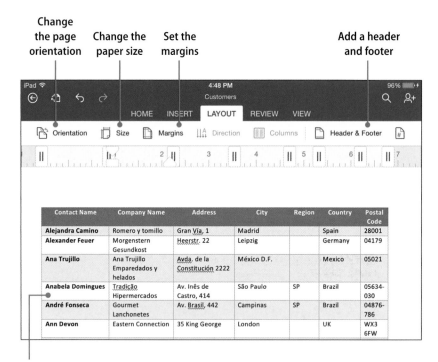

Build a table

In this chapter, you learn about creating tables to hold structured data, adding headers and footers to your documents, and working with page layout options such as margins, page orientation, and paper size.

→ Inserting a table into a Word document

→ Working with table rows and columns

→ Adding and populating document headers and footers

→ Choosing a page orientation and paper size

→ Setting the page margins

→ Adding footnotes and endnotes

Working with Page Layout and Design in Word

In the previous chapter, you dealt with Word at the "tree" level of words, sentences, and paragraphs. But getting more out of Word also requires that you deal with the program at the "forest" level of pages and documents. This means you need to get familiar with Word's page layout tools.

Page layout refers to how text and paragraphs are laid out on each page, and it involves building tables, adding headers and footers, setting margin sizes, specifying the page orientation, choosing the paper size, and so on. This chapter shows you how to work with these and other page layout features.

Building a Table

Most Word documents consist of text in the form of sentences and paragraphs. However, including lists of items in a document is common, particularly where each item in the list includes two or more details (which means a standard bulleted list won't do the job). For a short list with just a few details, the quickest way to add the list to a document is to type each item on its own line and press Tab between each detail. You could then add tab stops to the ruler (see Chapter 4, "Working with Text in Word") to line up the subitems into columns.

That works for simple items, but to construct a more complex list in the Word app, you can build a table, a rectangular structure with the following characteristics:

- Each item in the list gets its own horizontal rectangle called a *row*.

- Each set of details in the list gets its own vertical rectangle called a *column*.

- The rectangle formed by the intersection of a row and a column is called a *cell*, and you use the table cells to hold the data.

In other words, a Word table is similar to an Excel worksheet and an Access datasheet.

Insert a Table

Creating a table in Word involves inserting a default table and then formatting and editing that table to suit your needs.

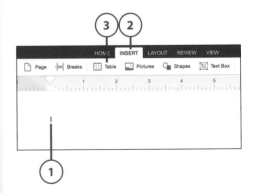

1. Tap where you want the table to appear.

2. Tap the Insert tab.

3. Tap Table. Word inserts a default table with three rows and three columns.

4. Tap inside a cell and then add the text that you want to store in the cell. Repeat for the other cells in the table.

You can set a column's width by dragging its width marker in the ruler

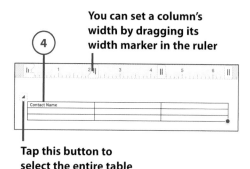

Tap this button to select the entire table

Displaying the Ruler

If you don't see the ruler, tap the View tab and then tap the Ruler switch to On.

>>>Go Further
CONVERTING TEXT TO A TABLE

If you already have a list where each column is separated by a tab, comma, or some other consistent character, you can convert that list to a table. Just select the list, tap the Insert tab, and then tap the Table command. Word examines the text and converts it into a table with the number of rows and columns determined by your data.

Select Table Elements

Before you can change the layout or formatting of a table, you need to select the part of the table you want to work with. Here are the techniques to use:

- **Select a cell**—Tap and hold the cell for a few seconds, release, and then tap Select.

- **Select two or more adjacent cells**—Select one of the cells and then drag the start and end selection handles to include the other cells.

- **Select a row**—Select any cell in the row and then extend the selection left and right to include the entire row.

- **Select two or more adjacent rows**—Select one of the rows and then extend the selection up and down to include the rows you want to work with.

- **Select a column**—Select any cell in the column and then extend the selection up and down to include the entire column.

- **Select two or more adjacent columns**—Select one of the columns and then extend the selection left and right to include the columns you want to work with.

- **Select the entire table**—Tap any cell in the table and then tap the Select Table button that appears slightly above and to the left of the table.

Format a Table

To change the formatting of the table cells, select the cells you want to work with and then use Word's standard formatting tools (font, paragraph, and so on). For more table-specific formatting, you can use the Table tab.

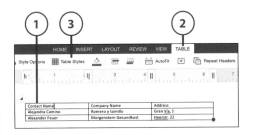

1. Tap inside the table.

2. Tap the Table tab.

3. Tap Table Styles.

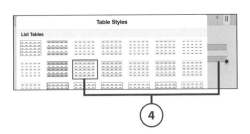

4. Tap the style you want to apply to the table.

5. Tap Style Options.

6. Tap Header Row to toggle header formatting on and off for the first row.

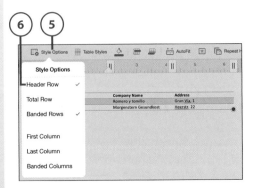

Header Formatting

In some table styles the first row is given darker shading, top and bottom borders, and a bold font, which helps distinguish the table headings from the regular table data.

7. Tap Total Row to toggle total formatting on and off for the bottom row.

8. Tap Banded Rows to toggle alternating formatting for all the rows.

9. Tap First Column to toggle special formatting on and off for the first column.

10. Tap Last Column to toggle special formatting on and off for the last column.

11. Tap Banded Columns to toggle alternating formatting for all the columns.

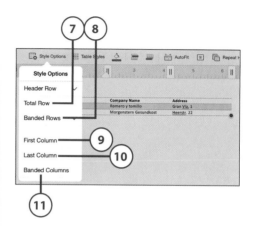

Insert New Rows

The default table comes with only three rows and three columns, so you usually have to add more data to a table. If you add new items to the table, you need to add more rows.

1. Tap inside an existing row.

Choosing the Row

You add a row either above or below whichever row you select, so be sure to tap the appropriate row.

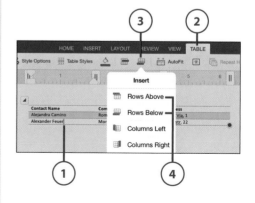

2. Tap the Table tab.

3. Tap Insert.

4. To add a new row above the current row, tap Rows Above; to add a new row below the current row, tap Rows Below.

>>>Go Further

INSERTING MULTIPLE ROWS

If you want to insert multiple rows, you can insert them all in one operation. To begin, select the same number of existing rows. For example, if you want to insert three rows into your table, select three existing rows. Again, you'll be inserting the new rows either above or below the selection, so select your rows accordingly. In the options that appear onscreen, tap Insert, and then tap either Rows Above or Rows Below.

Insert New Columns

If you need to add more details to each item in your table, you need to add more columns.

1. Tap inside an existing column.

Choosing the Column

You insert a column either to the left or to the right of whichever column you select, so be sure to tap the appropriate column.

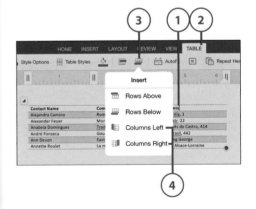

2. Tap the Table tab.

3. Tap Insert.

4. To add a new row above the current row, tap Rows Above; to add a new row below the current row, tap Rows Below.

>>>*Go Further*

INSERTING MULTIPLE COLUMNS

As with multiple rows (see "Insert New Rows,"), if you want to insert multiple columns, you can insert them all at once. To begin, select the same number of existing columns. For example, if you want to insert two columns into your table, select two existing columns. Again, you'll be inserting the new columns either to the left or to the right of the selection, so select your columns accordingly. In the options that appear onscreen, tap Insert, and then tap either Columns Left or Columns Right.

Delete Rows and Columns

If you find there's a part of your table you no longer need—for example, a cell, a row, or a column—you can delete it. You can delete multiple cells, rows, or columns, and, if necessary, you can also delete the entire table.

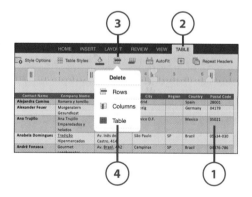

1. Select the table element you want to delete.

2. Tap the Table tab.

3. Tap Delete.

4. Tap the command that represents the type of table element you want to delete: Rows, Columns, or Table.

Selecting Elements for Deletion

If you want to delete a row or column, you need to only tap anywhere inside that row or column. If you want to delete multiple rows or columns, then you need to select at least one cell in each row or column. If you plan on deleting the entire table, you need to only tap anywhere inside the table.

Working with Headers and Footers

A header is a section that appears at the top of each page between the top margin and the first line of text. Any text, graphics, or properties you insert in any header appear at the top of every page in the document. Typical header contents include the document title and the date the document was created or modified.

A footer is a section that appears at the bottom of each page between the bottom margin and the last line of text. As with a header, anything you insert in any footer appears at the bottom of every page in the document. Typical footer contents include the page number and document filename.

Although in desktop Word you can add a wide variety of content to the header and footer, the Word app supports only the following:

- **Page numbers**—You can insert a special page number field, which shows the current page number.

- **Text**—You can type any text, such as a brief document description, a note to the reader, or your company name.

- **Picture or shape**—You can insert a photo or other image from your iPad or you can draw a shape.

Add a Header

You create a header by inserting a blank header and then adding page numbers, text, or images.

1. Tap the Layout tab.

2. Tap Header & Footer.

3. Tap Edit Header.

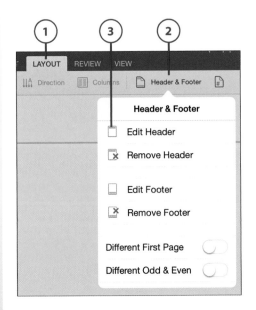

>>>Go Further
CREATING A UNIQUE FIRST-PAGE HEADER

By default, when you define the content for one header, Word displays the same content in every header in the document. However, situations may arise in which this default behavior is not what you want. One common situation is when you want to use a different header on the first page of a document. Another example is when you want to insert document instructions or notes in the first header, but you do not want that text repeated on every page.

For these kinds of situations, you can instruct Word that you want the first page's header to be different from the headers and footers in the rest of the document. You set this up by tapping the Layout tab's Header & Footer command and then tapping the Different First Page switch to On. Word changes the label of the first page header to First Page Header.

4. If you want to include a page number in your header, tap Page Numbers to open the Page Numbers dialog.

5. Tap the Numbering switch to On.

6. If you don't want the page number to appear in the first page header, tap the Show # on First Page switch to Off.

7. Tap Position and then tap Top of Page.

8. Tap Alignment and then tap how you want the page numbers aligned within the header: Left, Center, Right, Inside, or Outside.

9. Tap Format and then tap the number style you want to use.

10. Tap outside the Page Numbers dialog to close it.

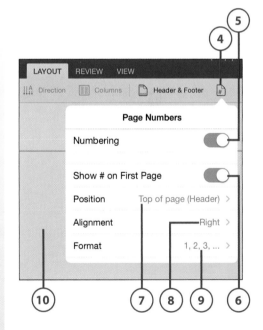

Inside or Outside Page Numbers

The Inside and Outside page number alignments set up different page number positions for odd and even pages. The Outside alignment adds the page number to the left on even pages and to the right on odd pages (as you see in this book), whereas Inside alignment adds the page number to the right on even pages and to the left on odd pages.

11. To add text, tap inside the header and then type your text.

12. If you want to include an image from your iPad, tap Insert and then tap Pictures. See "Insert a Picture" in Chapter 3, "Working with Office for iPad Graphics."

13. If you want to draw a shape, tap Insert and then tap Shapes. See "Inserting Any Other Shape" in Chapter 3.

14. When you're done, tap the Close button in the Header label.

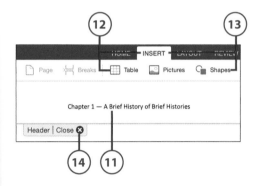

>>>Go Further
CREATING UNIQUE ODD AND EVEN PAGE HEADERS

Many documents require different layouts for the header on odd and even pages. A good example is the book you are holding. Notice that the even page header has the page number on the left, followed by the current chapter number and name, while the odd page header has the page number on the right, preceded by the current section name.

To handle this type of situation, you can configure your document with different odd and even page headers and footers by tapping the Layout tab's Header & Footer command and then tapping the Different Odd & Even switch to On. Word changes the labels of the page headers to Even Page Header and Odd Page Header.

Change the Paper Size

Word assumes that you'll be printing your documents (on your PC) on standard letter-size paper, which is 8.5 inches by 11 inches. If you plan on using a different paper size, then you need to let Word know what you will be using so that it can print the document correctly.

1. Tap the Layout tab.

2. Tap Size.

3. Tap a paper size.

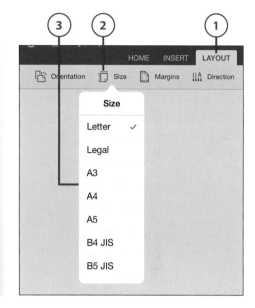

>>>Go Further
PRINTING ON THE EDGE

Getting the proper printout isn't the only reason for configuring Word to use a different page size. An old trick is to instruct Word you are using a larger paper size than you actually are. Word will then print the page as if you're using the larger size, which with some experimentation means you can get Word to print right to (or pretty close to) the edge of a regular sheet of paper or an envelope.

Set the Margins

One of the most common page layout changes is to adjust the margins, the blank space to the left, right, above, and below the document text (including the header and footer). The standard margins are 1 inch on all sides. Decreasing the margins fits more text on each page (which is useful when printing a long document), but it can also make the printout look cluttered and uninviting. If you increase the margins, you get less text on each page, but the added whitespace can make the document look more appealing.

You can set specific margin sizes for the Top, Bottom, Left, and Right margins, and you can also specify where you want Word to apply the new margins: to the whole document or from the insertion point forward.

1. Tap the Layout tab.

2. Tap Margin.

3. Tap a margin setting.

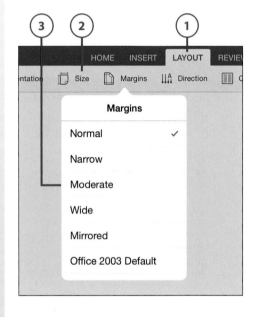

>>>Go Further

WORD'S MARGIN SETTINGS

Word's named margin settings aren't very helpful if you need to know the specific margin sizes. Here's a summary:

Setting	Top	Bottom	Left	Right
Normal	1"	1"	1"	1"
Narrow	0.5"	0.5"	0.5"	0.5"
Moderate	1"	1"	0.75"	0.75"
Wide	1"	1"	2"	2"
Office 2003 Default	1"	1"	1.25"	1.25"

For the Mirrored setting, Word uses 1-inch top and bottom margins, but different left and right margins for odd and even pages. The inside margin (that is, the right margin on an even page and the left margin on an odd page) is set to 1.25 inches, whereas the outside margin (that is, the left margin on an even page and the right margin on an odd page) is set to 1 inch.

Add a Page Break

If you have a paragraph that must begin at the top of a page, you can ensure that happens by inserting a page break just before that paragraph.

1. Tap at the beginning of the paragraph that you want to appear on a new page.

2. Tap the Insert tab.

3. Tap Breaks.

4. Tap Page.

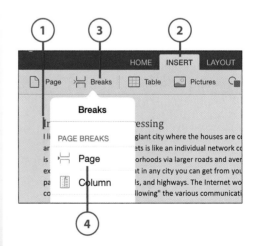

Understanding Sections

In Word-related training sessions and question-and-answer periods, some of the most common complaints and queries center on using multiple page layouts in a single document:

- How can I have different headers (or footers) for different parts of a document?

- I have a long table on one page. How can I set up that one page with landscape orientation?

- Can I switch from a two-column layout to a three-column layout for part of a document?

Most people end up splitting a single document into multiple documents to accomplish these and similar tasks. However, you do not have to break up your document just because you want to break up the page layout. The secret to doing this is the section, a document part that stores page layout options such as the following:

- Margins

- Page size and page orientation

- Headers and footers

- Columns

- Line numbering

- Footnotes and endnotes

Add a Section Break

When you create a document, Word gives it a single section that comprises the entire document. However, you are free to create multiple sections within a single document, and you can then apply separate page layout formatting to each section. The transition from one section to another is called a section break.

1. Tap where you want the new section to begin.

2. Tap the Insert tab.

3. Tap Breaks.

4. Tap a section break.

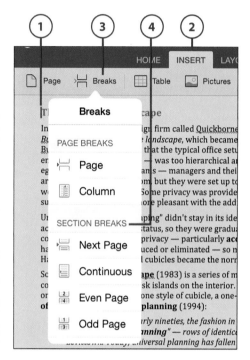

>>>Go Further
WORD'S SECTION BREAKS

Word for iPad offers four types of section breaks:

• **Next Page**—Starts a new section on a new page

• **Continuous**—Starts a new section at the insertion point (does not add a page break)

• **Even Page**—Starts a new section on the next even numbered page

• **Odd Page**—Starts a new section on the next odd numbered page

Display Text in Columns

If you put together a brochure, newsletter, or any document where you want to mimic the layout of a newspaper or magazine, you probably want your text to appear in two or more columns. When you use columns, as the text in the first column reaches the bottom of the page, it continues at the top of the next column. It's only when the text reaches the bottom of the last column that it continues on the next page.

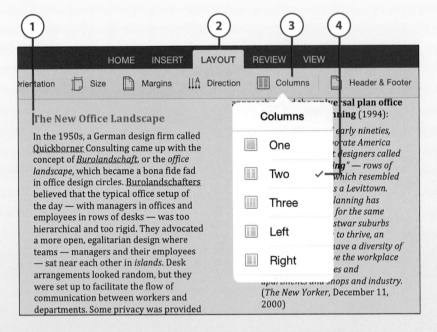

1. Tap where you want to convert the text to columns.

Positioning the Insertion Point for Columns

If your document has only one section and you want to use columns for the entire document, position the insertion point anywhere within the document. If your document has multiple sections and you want to use columns for a single section, position the insertion point anywhere within that section. If your document has multiple sections and you want to use columns for the entire document, select the entire document.

2. Tap the Layout tab.

3. Tap Columns.

4. Tap a column setting.

>>>*Go Further*
WORD'S COLUMN SETTINGS

Word for iPad offers five default column settings:

- **One**—Reverts the text to a single column

- **Two**—Splits the text into two columns of the same width

- **Three**—Splits the text into three columns of the same width

- **Left**—Splits the text into two columns, with a narrow column on the left and a wide column on the right

- **Right**—Splits the text into two columns, with a narrow column on the right and a wide column on the left

Adding Footnotes

A footnote is a short note at the bottom of a page that provides extra information about something mentioned in the regular text on that page. Word indicates a footnote with a reference mark, a number or other symbol that appears as a superscript in both the regular text and in a special footnote box at the bottom of the page.

Word makes working with footnotes and endnotes a breeze. Not only are they easy to insert, but Word also keeps track of the reference marks and updates the numbers (or whatever) automatically no matter where you insert new notes in the document.

Insert a Footnote

The footnote appears at the bottom of the current page and uses Arabic numerals (1, 2, 3, and so on) as the reference marks.

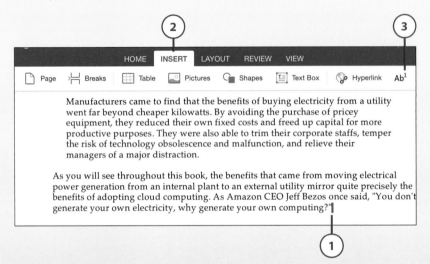

1. Tap where you want the footnote reference mark to appear.

2. Tap the Insert tab.

3. Tap Insert Footnote.

> As you will see throughout this book, the benefits that came from moving electrical power generation from an internal plant to an external utility mirror quite precisely the benefits of adopting cloud computing. As Amazon CEO Jeff Bezos once said, "You don't generate your own electricity, why generate your own computing?"[1]
>
> So *instant-on* describes computing services that are available immediately (or, at least, extremely quickly), just like electrical power or other utilities, such as water and natural gas. Do you have instant-on IT in your business? Probably not. It's more likely that your IT products are "eventually on" where they go through the same interminable process
>
> ——————————
> [1] **Jeff Bezos,** as quoted in Spencer Reiss, *Cloud Computing. Available at Amazon.com Today,* Wired, http://www.wired.com/techbiz/it/magazine/16-05/mf_amazon (April 21, 2008).

**Word inserts the reference mark
in the text and in the note area**

4. Type your note text.

Create formulas

Add functions
to formulas

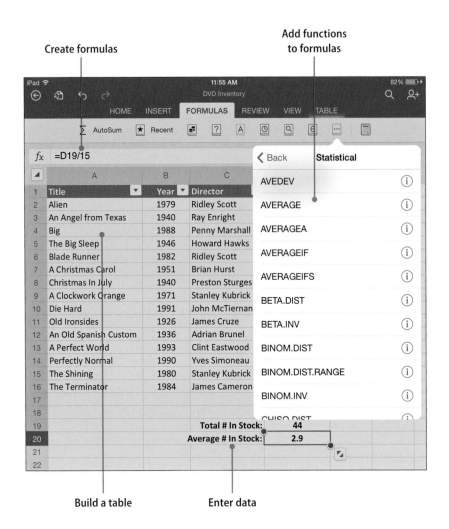

Build a table

Enter data

In this chapter, you learn about entering data into an Excel worksheet, building formulas, working with functions, and storing data in tables.

→ Entering numbers, text, dates, and times

→ Editing cell data

→ Building formulas to add calculations to a worksheet

→ Creating and working with Excel tables

6

Entering Excel Data

If you've never used a spreadsheet before, Excel may seem intimidating and getting it to do anything useful may seem like a daunting task. However, a spreadsheet is really just a fancy electronic version of a numeric scratch pad. With the latter, you write down a few numbers and then use elementary school techniques to calculate a result. At its most basic level, an Excel worksheet is much the same: You type one or more values and then you create a formula that calculates a result.

The first part of this basic Excel method is entering your worksheet data, and that's what this chapter is all about. You learn the best ways to get your data into the worksheet, some tips and tricks for easier data entry, how to build formulas, and how to use tables to make your data easier to read and understand.

Understanding Worksheet Cells and Data

A worksheet is a rectangular arrangement of rows and columns. The rows are numbered, where the topmost row is 1, the row below it is 2, and so on all the way to 1,048,576. (Although, as you can imagine, worksheets that use more than a million rows are quite rare!) The columns are labeled with letters, where A is the leftmost column, the next column is B, and so on. After column Z come columns AA, AB, and so on, all the way up to XFD; that's 16,384 columns in all.

The intersection of each row and column is called a cell, and each cell has a unique address that combines its column letter (or letters) and row number. For example, the upper-left cell in a worksheet is at the intersection of column A and row 1, so its address is A1. When you tap a cell, it becomes the active cell—which Excel designates by surrounding the cell with a heavy border and by displaying a small square in the lower-right corner—and its address appears in the Name box, which is located just above column A.

You use these worksheet cells to enter your data, which you learn more about in the next few sections. For now, you should know that worksheet cells can hold four kinds of data:

- **Numbers**—These entries can be dollar values, weights, interest rates, or any other numerical quantity.

- **Text**—These entries are usually labels such as *August Sales* or *Territory* that make a worksheet easier to read, but they can also be text/number combinations for items such as phone numbers and account codes.

- **Dates and times**—These entries are specific dates (such as 8/23/2014), specific times (such as 9:05 a.m.), or combinations of the two. You mostly use dates (and, to a lesser extent, times) in tables and lists to record when something took place, although Excel also lets you calculate with dates and times.

- **Formulas**—These are calculations involving two or more values, such as 2*5 or A1+A2+A3. See the "Working with Formulas and Functions" section later in this chapter.

Working with Numbers

Worksheets are all about numbers. You add them together, subtract them, take their average, or perform any number of mathematical operations on them. Excel recognizes that you're entering a number if you start the entry with a decimal point (.), a plus sign (+), a minus sign (–), or a dollar sign ($). Here are some other rules for entering numbers:

- You can enter percentages by following the number with a percent sign (%). Excel stores the number as a decimal. For example, the entry **15%** is stored as 0.15.

- You can use scientific notation when entering numbers. For example, to enter the number 3,879,000,000, you could enter **3.879E+09**.

- You can also use parentheses to indicate a negative number. If you make an entry such as **(125)**, Excel assumes you mean negative 125.

- You can enter commas to separate thousands, but you have to make sure that each comma appears in the appropriate place. Excel will interpret an entry such as **12,34** as text.

- If you want to enter a fraction, you need to type an integer, a space, and then the fraction (**5 1/8**, for example). This is true even if you're entering only the fractional part; in this case, you need to type a zero, a space, and then the fraction or else Excel will interpret the entry as a date. For example, **0 1/8** is the fraction one-eighth, but **1/8** is January 8.

Working with Text

In Excel, text entries can include any combination of letters, symbols, and numbers. Although text is sometimes used as data, you'll find that you mostly use text to describe the contents of your worksheets. This is very important because even a modest-sized spreadsheet can become a confusing jumble of numbers without some kind of guideline to keep things straight. There is no practical limit on the length of text entries (they can be up to 32,767 characters long!), but in general, you shouldn't use anything too fancy or elaborate; a simple phrase such as Monthly Expenses or Payment Date will usually suffice.

Working with Dates and Times

Excel uses serial numbers to represent specific dates and times. To get a date serial number, Excel uses December 31, 1899, as an arbitrary starting point and counts the number of days that have passed since then. For example, the date serial number for January 1, 1900, is 1; for January 2, 1900, it is 2; and so on. Table 6.1 displays some examples of date serial numbers.

Table 6.1   Examples of Date Serial Numbers

Serial Number	Date
366	December 31, 1900
16229	June 6, 1944
42004	December 31, 2013

To get a time serial number, Excel expresses time as a decimal fraction of the 24-hour day to get a number between 0 and 1. The starting point, midnight, is given the value 0, so noon—halfway through the day—has a serial number of 0.5. Table 6.2 displays some examples of time serial numbers.

Table 6.2   Examples of Time Serial Numbers

Serial Number	Time
0.25	6:00:00 AM
0.375	9:00:00 AM
0.70833	5:00:00 PM
.99999	11:59:59 PM

You can combine the two types of serial numbers. For example, 42004.5 represents noon on December 31, 2013.

The advantage of using serial numbers in this way is that it makes calculations involving dates and times very easy. A date or time is really just a number, so any mathematical operation you can perform on a number you can also perform on a date. This is invaluable for worksheets that track delivery times, monitor accounts receivable or accounts payable aging, calculate invoice discount dates, and so on.

Although it's true that the serial numbers make it easier for the computer to manipulate dates and times, it's not the best format for humans to comprehend. For example, the number 25,404.95555 is meaningless, but the moment it represents (July 20, 1969, at 10:56 p.m. EDT) is one of the great moments in history (the Apollo 11 moon landing). Fortunately, Excel takes care of the conversion between these formats so that you never have to worry about it.

To enter a date or time, use any of the formats outlined in Table 6.3.

Table 6.3 Excel Date and Time Formats

Format	Example
m/d	8/23
m/d/yy	8/23/14
d-mmm	23-Aug (Excel assumes the current year.)
d-mmm-yy	23-Aug-14
mmm-yy	Aug-14 (Excel assumes the first day of the month.)
mmmm-yy	August-14
mmmm d, yyyy	August 23, 2014
dddd, mmmm d, yyyy	Monday, August 23, 2014
h:mm AM/PM	3:10 PM
h:mm:ss AM/PM	3:10:45 PM
h:mm	15:10
h:mm:ss	15:10:45
mm:ss.0	10:45.7
m/d/yy h:mm AM/PM	8/23/14 3:10 PM
m/d/yy h:mm	8/23/14 15:10

Entering and Editing Data

A spreadsheet is only as useful—and as accurate—as the data it contains. Even a small mistake can render your results meaningless. So the first rule of good spreadsheet style is to enter and edit your data carefully.

Enter Cell Data

If you're new to spreadsheet work, you'll no doubt be pleased to hear that entering data into a worksheet cell is straightforward.

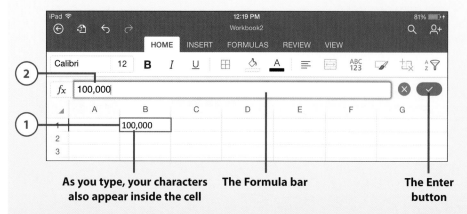

As you type, your characters also appear inside the cell   **The Formula bar**   **The Enter button**

1. Double-tap the cell you want to use to enter your data. Excel activates the Formula bar.

2. Type your data.

Tap here to switch between numbers and letters

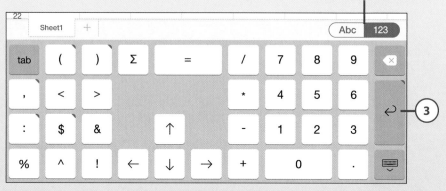

3. When your entry is complete, tap the Return key. Excel moves the active cell to the cell below. If you don't want the active cell to move after you confirm your entry, tap the Enter button, instead.

Confirming Data Entry with the Arrow Keys

You can also confirm your entry by tapping any of the arrow keys or by tapping another cell. The active cell moves either in the direction of the arrow or to the cell you tapped. This feature is handy if you have, say, a lengthy row of data to type in. By tapping (in this case) the right arrow key to confirm each entry, you automatically move the active cell along the row.

Edit Cell Data

If you make a mistake when entering data or you have to update the contents of a cell, you need to edit the cell to get the correct value. If you want to replace the entire cell contents, follow the steps in the previous section. This section shows you how to make changes to a cell's existing content.

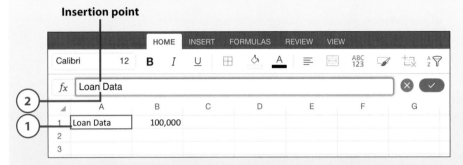

Insertion point

1. Double-tap the cell you want to edit. Excel displays and selects the cell data in the Formula bar.

2. Tap inside the Formula bar at the spot where you want to edit the data. The insertion point appears inside the Formula bar at the end of the entry.

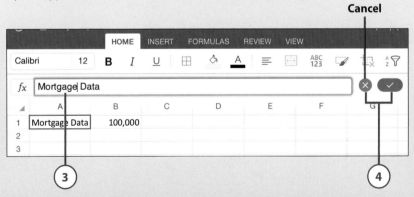

Cancel

3. Edit the contents of the cell.

4. Confirm your changes by tapping Enter. To cancel the edit without confirming your changes, tap Cancel, instead.

Working with Formulas and Functions

Any worksheet is merely a collection of numbers and text until you define some kind of relationship between the various entries. You do this by creating formulas that perform calculations and produce results. This section takes you through some formula basics and then shows you how to build your own formulas.

Excel divides formulas into three main groups: arithmetic, comparison, and text. Each group has its own set of operators, and you use each group in different ways.

Let's start with arithmetic formulas, which are by far the most common type of formula. They combine numbers, cell addresses, and function results with mathematic operators to perform calculations. Table 6.4 summarizes the mathematic operators used in arithmetic formulas.

Table 6.4   The Arithmetic Operators

Operator	Name	Example	Result
+	Addition	=10+5	15
−	Subtraction	=10-5	5
−	Negation	=−10	−10
*	Multiplication	=10*5	50
/	Division	=10/5	2
%	Percentage	=10%	.1
^	Exponentiation	=10^5	100,000

Most of the operators in Table 6.4 are straightforward, but the exponentiation operator may require further explanation. The formula =x^y means that the value x is raised to the power y. For example, =3^2 produces the result 9 (that is, 3*3=9). Similarly, =2^4 produces 16 (that is, 2*2*2*2=16).

A comparison formula is a statement that compares two or more numbers, text strings, cell contents, or function results. If the statement is true, the result of the formula is given the logical value TRUE (which is equivalent to 1). If the statement is false, the formula returns the logical value FALSE (which is equivalent to 0). Table 6.5 summarizes the operators you can use in comparison formulas.

Table 6.5   Comparison Formula Operators

Operator	Name	Example	Result
=	Equal to	=10=5	FALSE
>	Greater than	=10>5	TRUE
<	Less than	=10<5	FALSE
>=	Greater than or equal to	="a">="b"	FALSE
<=	Less than or equal to	="a"<="b"	TRUE
<>	Not equal to	="a"<>"b"	TRUE

There are many uses for comparison formulas. For example, you could determine whether to pay a salesperson a bonus by using a comparison formula to compare the person's actual sales with a predetermined quota. If the sales are greater than the quota, the salesperson is awarded the bonus. Another example is credit collection. If the amount a customer owes is, say, more than 150 days past due, then you might send the receivable to a collection agency.

Build a Formula

Building a formula is similar to entering data into a cell, with the exception that all Excel formulas must begin with an equal sign (=).

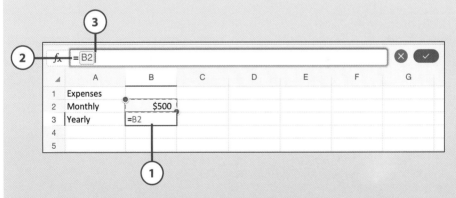

1. Double-tap the cell you want to use for the formula.

2. Type an equal sign (=).

3. Enter a value, cell reference, range, range name, or function name.

Tapping to Enter a Cell Address

When entering a cell reference in a formula, you could just type in the cell address, but it's often faster and more accurate to let Excel do the work by tapping the cell. The address appears automatically in the formula at the insertion point.

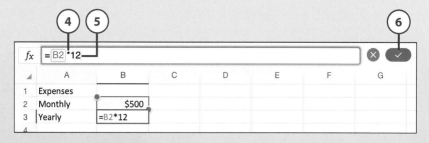

4. Enter an operator (such as + or *).

5. Repeat Steps 3 and 4 until the formula is complete.

6. Tap the Enter button (or tap the Return key) to accept the formula.

>>>Go Further

CONTROLLING THE ORDER OF CALCULATION

When you use the operators listed earlier in Tables 6.4 and 6.5, be aware that Excel processes the operators not only from left to right, but also by giving some operators precedence over others. For example, Excel always performs multiplication and division before it performs addition and subtraction. In some cases, you might need to control the order of calculation so that, say, Excel performs an addition operation before it performs a multiplication. To do this, enclose the operation you want performed first in parentheses. Excel always calculates expressions enclosed in parentheses first, so you can use this technique to force Excel to calculate your formulas in whatever order you require.

Understanding Functions

Consider the following scenario: You want to deposit a specific amount of money in an investment that earns a particular rate of interest over a particular number of years. Assuming you start at zero, how much will that investment be worth at the end of the term? Given a present value (represented by *pv*), a regular payment (*pmt*), an annual interest rate (*rate*), and some number of years (*nper*), here's the formula that calculates the future value of the investment:

```
pv(1 + rate) ^ nper + pmt * (((1 + rate) ^ nper) - 1) / rate
```

That's a *really* complex formula, but this complexity wouldn't be a big deal if this formula were obscure or rarely used. However, calculating the future value of an investment is one of the most common Excel chores. (It is, for example, the central calculation in most retirement planning models.) Having to type such a formula once is bad enough, but it is one you may need dozens of times. Clearly, entering such a formula by hand so many times is both time-consuming and prone to errors.

Fortunately, Excel offers a solution: a worksheet function called FV(), which reduces the earlier formula to the following:

```
fv(rate, nper, pmt, pv)
```

Not only is this formula simpler to use and faster to type, you also don't have to memorize anything other than the function name because, as you'll soon see, Excel shows you the full function syntax (that is, the list of arguments and the order in which they appear) as you type it.

In general, a function is a predefined formula that calculates a result based on one or more arguments, which are the function's input values (such as *rate* and *nper* in the FV() example). See Appendix A, "Excel Worksheet Function Reference," for a complete list of the worksheet functions that are available in Excel for iPad.

For most functions, you see two types of argument:

- **Required**—These arguments are shown in bold text. You must provide a value for each of these arguments; otherwise, Excel will generate an error instead of the function result.

- **Optional**—These arguments appear in regular text; you can leave them out if your formula doesn't need them.

Functions not only simplify complex mathematical formulas, but they also enable you to perform powerful calculations such as statistical correlation, the number of workdays between two dates, and square roots.

Add a Function to a Formula

The quickest way to include a function in a formula is to type the function and its arguments directly into the cell.

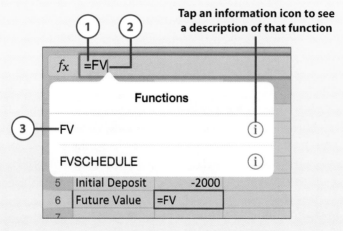

Tap an information icon to see a description of that function

1. Enter your formula up to the point where you want to include the function.

2. Begin typing the function name. As you type, Excel displays a list of function names that begin with what you have typed so far.

3. Tap the function you want to use. Excel adds the function name and displays its syntax.

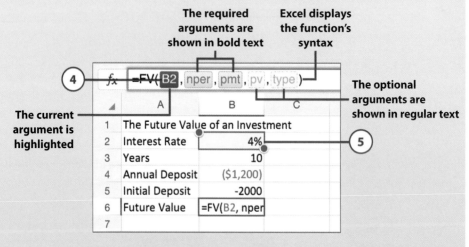

The required arguments are shown in bold text

Excel displays the function's syntax

The current argument is highlighted

The optional arguments are shown in regular text

4. Tap the argument you want to add.

5. Enter the argument value, either by typing the value or by tapping a cell, if applicable.

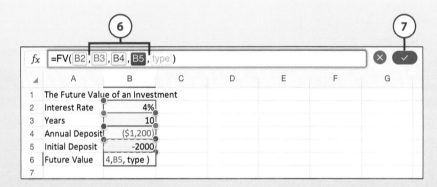

6. Repeat Steps 4 and 5 to specify all the required arguments, as well as any optional arguments you need for your formula.

7. Tap the Enter button (or tap the Return key). Excel enters the formula and displays the formula result in the cell.

Cell Arguments Are Color-Coded

To make it easier to check and troubleshoot your formulas, Excel color-codes the arguments that reference worksheet cells and displays these colors whenever you edit the formula. For example, if the first argument references cell B2, that cell appears with a blue background, and the argument appears with the same blue background, as well as blue text.

Select a Function from a List

If you're not sure of the name of the function you need or what functions are available, Excel's Formulas tab presents several function lists divided into seven categories: Financial, Logical, Text, Date and Time, Lookup and Reference, Math and Trigonometry, and More. This last category includes four subcategories: Statistical, Engineering, Info, and Database.

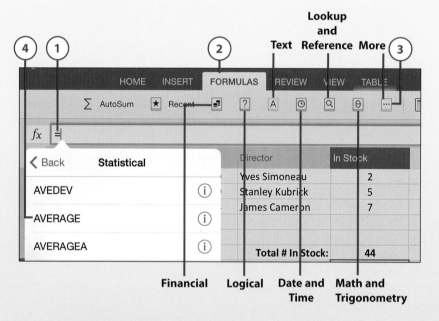

1. Enter your formula up to the point where you want to include the function.

2. Tap the Formulas tab.

3. Tap a function category.

4. Tap the function you want to use. Excel adds the function to the formula. Follow the steps in the "Add a Function to a Formula" section to specify the function arguments and complete your formula.

The Most Recently Used List

Excel maintains a list of the last few functions you have used. If the function you want is one that you used recently, tap the Formulas tab, tap Recent, and then use the Recently Used Functions list to tap the function.

Building a Table

Excel's forte is spreadsheet work, of course, but its row-and-column layout also makes it a natural database manager. In Excel, a table is a collection of related information with an organizational structure that makes it easy to find or extract data from its contents. Specifically, a table is a collection of cells that has the following properties:

- **Field**—A single type of information, such as a name, an address, or a phone number. In Excel tables, each column is a field.

- **Field value**—A single item in a field. In an Excel table, the field values are the individual cells.

- **Field name**—A unique name you assign to every table field (worksheet column). These names are always found in the first row of the table.

- **Record**—A collection of associated field values. In Excel tables, each row is a record.

Converting Cells to a Table

Excel has a number of commands that enable you to work efficiently with table data. To take advantage of these commands, you must convert your data from normal cells to a table.

1. Tap any cell within the group of cells that you want to convert to a table.

2. Tap the Insert tab.

3. Tap Table. Excel converts the cells to a table.

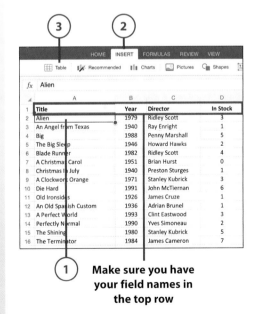

Make sure you have your field names in the top row

Select Table Elements

Before you can change the layout or formatting of a table, you need to select the part of the table you want to work with. Here are the techniques to use:

- **Select a cell**—Tap and hold the cell for a few seconds, release, and then tap Select.

- **Select two or more adjacent cells**—Select one of the cells, and then drag the start and end selection handles to include the other cells.

- **Select a row**—Select any cell in the row, and then extend the selection left and right to include the entire row.

- **Select two or more adjacent rows**—Select one of the rows, and then extend the selection up and down to include the rows you want to work with.

- **Select a column**—Select any cell in the column, and then extend the selection up and down to include the entire column.

- **Select two or more adjacent columns**—Select one of the columns and then extend the selection left and right to include the columns you want to work with.

- **Select the entire table**—Tap any cell in the table, and then tap the Select Table button that appears slightly above and to the left of the table.

Format a Table

To change the formatting of the table cells, select the cells you want to work with and then use Excel's standard formatting tools (font, paragraph, and so on). For more table-specific formatting, you can use the Table tab.

1. Tap inside the table.

2. Tap the Table tab.

3. Tap Table Styles.

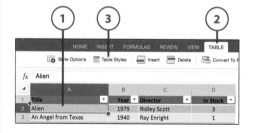

4. Tap the style you want to apply to the table.

5. Tap Style Options.

6. Tap Header Row to toggle header formatting on and off for the first row.

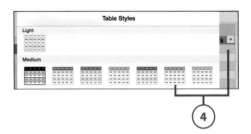

Header Formatting

In some table styles the first row is given darker shading, top and bottom borders, and a bold font, which helps distinguish the table headings from the regular table data.

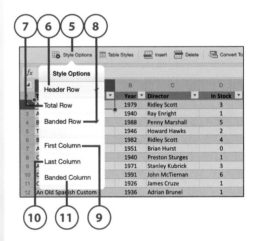

7. Tap Total Row to toggle total formatting on and off for the bottom row.

8. Tap Banded Rows to toggle alternating formatting for all the rows.

9. Tap First Column to toggle special formatting on and off for the first column.

10. Tap Last Column to toggle special formatting on and off for the last column.

11. Tap Banded Columns to toggle alternating formatting for all the columns.

Insert New Rows

Data tends to increase over time, so you'll usually have to add more data to a table. If you're adding new items to the table, you need to add more rows.

1. Tap the existing row above which you want the new row to appear.

Adding a Row at the End

Excel allows you to add a row only above an existing row, with one exception. If you tap a cell in the bottom row of the table, you can add a row either above or below that row, and you'd choose the latter if you wanted to add your new row to the bottom of the table.

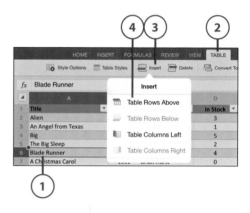

2. Tap the Table tab.

3. Tap Insert.

4. Tap Table Rows Above. (If you selected a cell in the bottom row in Step 1, you can also tap Table Rows Below.)

>>>Go Further
INSERTING MULTIPLE ROWS

If you want to insert multiple rows, you can insert them all in one operation. To begin, select the same number of existing rows. For example, if you want to insert three rows into your table, select three existing rows. In the options that appear onscreen, tap Insert, and then tap Rows Above.

Insert New Columns

If you need to add more details to each item in your table, you need to add more columns.

1. Tap the existing column to the left of which you want to add the new column.

Adding a Column at the End

Excel allows you to add a column only to the left of an existing column, with one exception. If you tap a cell in the rightmost column of the table, you can add a column either to the left or to the right of that column, and you'd choose the latter if you wanted to add your new column to the end of the table.

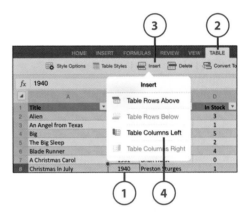

2. Tap the Table tab.

3. Tap Insert.

4. Tap Table Columns Left. (If you selected a cell in the rightmost column in Step 1, you can also tap Table Columns Right.)

>>>Go Further
INSERTING MULTIPLE COLUMNS

If you want to insert multiple columns, you can insert them all at once. To begin, select the same number of existing columns. For example, if you want to insert two columns into your table, select two existing columns. In the options that appear onscreen, tap Insert, and then tap Columns Left.

Delete Rows and Columns

If you find there's a part of your table you no longer need—for example, a cell, a row, or a column—you can delete it. You can delete one or more rows or columns.

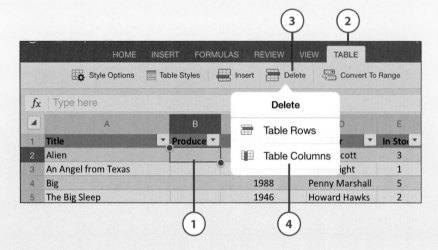

1. Select the table element you want to delete.

Selecting Elements for Deletion

If you want to delete a row or column, you need only to tap anywhere inside that row or column. If you want to delete multiple rows or columns, then you need to select at least one cell in each row or column.

2. Tap the Table tab.

3. Tap Delete.

4. Tap the command that represents the type of table element you want to delete: Table Rows or Table Columns.

Sorting a Table

One of the advantages of using a table is that you can rearrange the records so that they're sorted alphabetically or numerically. Sorting enables you to view the data in order by customer name, account number, part number, or any other field.

Excel offers two kinds of sorts:

- **Ascending**—This type of sort arranges the items in a field from smallest to largest if the field is numeric, from A to Z if the field is text, and from oldest to newest if the field contains date or time data.

- **Descending**—This sort type arranges the items in a field from largest to smallest if the field contains numbers, from Z to A if the field contains text, and from newest to oldest if the field contains dates or times.

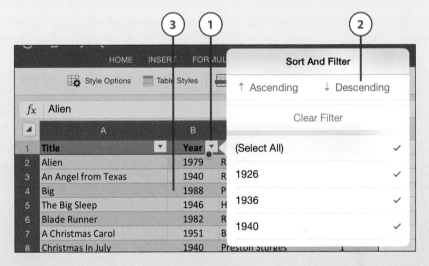

1. Tap the Sort and Filter button (the drop-down arrow that appears beside the field header) for the field you want to use for the sort.

2. Tap either Ascending or Descending.

3. Tap outside the Sort and Filter dialog to close it.

Filtering a Table

One of the biggest problems with large tables is that it's often hard to find and extract the data you need. Sorting can help, but in the end, you're still working with the entire table. You need a way to define the data that you want to work with and then have Excel display only those records onscreen. This is called filtering your data, and Excel's Filter feature makes filtering subsets of your data as easy as selecting and deselecting items using the filter list, a collection of the unique values in the field. When you deselect an item, Excel temporarily hides all the table records that include that item in the field.

To indicate that a field is filtered, Excel adds a funnel icon to the field's Sort and Filter button

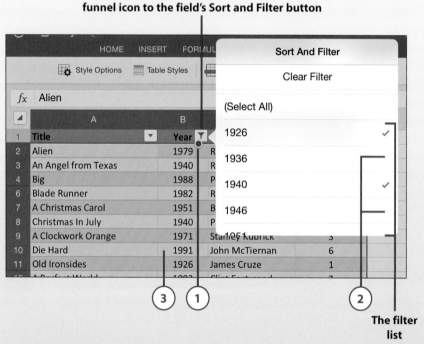

The filter list

1. Tap the Sort and Filter button for the field you want to use for the filter. Excel displays the field's filter list.

2. Deselect each item that you want to hide in the table.

3. Tap outside the Sort and Filter dialog to close it.

Restoring Filtered Items

To add the filtered items back into the table, tap the field's Sort and Filter button and then tap Clear Filter.

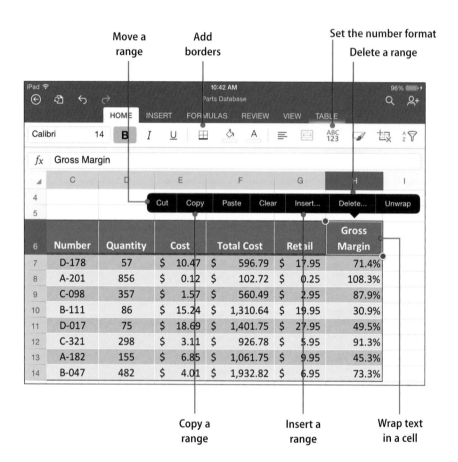

Move a range

Add borders

Set the number format

Delete a range

Copy a range

Insert a range

Wrap text in a cell

In this chapter, you learn about techniques for working with Excel ranges, including selecting, filling, copying, moving, inserting, deleting, and formatting ranges.

→ Selecting ranges
→ Automatically filling a range with data
→ Copying, moving, inserting, and deleting ranges
→ Applying formatting to a range

Getting More Out of Excel Ranges

For small worksheets, working with individual cells doesn't usually present a problem. However, as your worksheets get larger, you'll find that performing operations cell by cell wastes both time and energy. To overcome this, Excel lets you work with multiple cells in a single operation. You can then move, copy, delete, or format the cells as a group.

A group of related cells is called a range. A range can be as small as a single cell and as large as an entire spreadsheet. Most ranges are rectangular groups of adjacent cells. Rectangular ranges, like individual cells, have an address, and this address is given in terms of range coordinates. Range coordinates have the form UL:LR where UL is the address of the cell in the upper-left corner of the range and LR is the address of the cell in the lower-right corner of the range (for example, A1:C5 and D7:G15).

This chapter shows you how to select ranges in Excel on the iPad, and then how to work with ranges by filling them with data, copying and moving them, inserting and deleting them, and formatting them.

Selecting a Range

Ranges speed up your work by enabling you to perform operations or define functions on many cells at once instead of one at a time. For example, suppose you want to copy a large section of a worksheet to another file. If you work on individual cells, you might have to perform the copy procedure dozens of times. However, by creating a range that covers the entire section, you could do it with a single copy command.

Similarly, suppose you want to know the average of a column of numbers running from B1 to B50. You could enter all 50 numbers as arguments in Excel's AVERAGE() function, but typing AVERAGE(B1:B50) is decidedly quicker.

Select a Range on a Touchscreen

Because you're using Excel on a touch-screen device, you can use gestures to select a range.

1. Tap the first cell in the range you want to select. This is usually the cell in the upper-left corner of the range.

2. Tap and drag the end selection handle down (if you want to include multiple rows in the range) or to the right (to include multiple columns). As you drag the handle, Excel selects the cells. When you release the screen, Excel displays the edit menu, which you can use to work with the selected range.

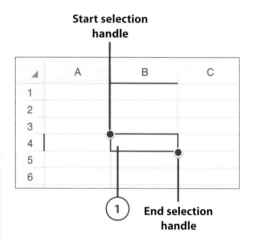

Start selection handle

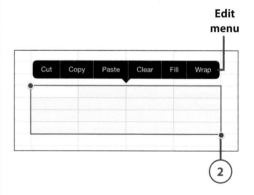

End selection handle

Edit menu

Selecting Entire Rows or Columns

To select an entire row, tap the row's heading. If you want to select multiple rows, tap and drag the selection handles left or right. To select an entire column, tap the column's heading. If you want to select multiple columns, tap and drag the selection handles up or down.

Working with Excel Ranges

After you select a range, you need to do something with it. What can you do with a range? A better question is what can't you do with a range? You'll find that most of the Excel tasks you perform will involve ranges in some form or another. The next few sections show you only some of the most common range chores, including filling, copying, moving, inserting, and deleting ranges.

Fill a Range with a Specific Value

You might occasionally need to fill a range with a particular value. For example, you might want to populate a range with a number for testing purposes, or you might need a value repeated across a range. Rather than type the value in by hand for each cell, you can use Excel's Fill tool to fill the range quickly.

1. Use the first cell of the range to enter the value you want to repeat.

2. Tap the cell that contains the value. Excel displays the Edit menu.

3. Tap Fill. Excel adds a Fill Down handle to the bottom edge of the cell and a Fill Right handle to the right edge of the cell.

4. Tap and drag the Fill Down handle down to include the range you want to fill. When you release the handle, Excel fills the range with the initial value.

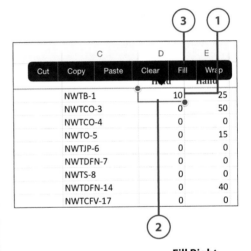

Fill Right handle

Fill Down handle

Filling Right

If you want to fill the value across columns, instead, tap and drag the Fill Right handle to the right to include the range you want to fill.

Fill a Range with a Series of Values

Worksheets often use text series (such as January, February, March; or Sunday, Monday, Tuesday) and numeric series (such as 1, 3, 5; or 2014, 2015, 2016). Instead of entering these series by hand, you can use Excel's Fill handles to create them automatically.

1. Use the first few cells of the range to enter the opening values of the series you want to repeat.

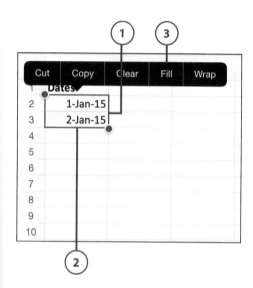

Setting the Series Pattern

The number of initial series values you need to enter depends on the pattern you want to use. Most patterns can be shown with just two values. If your fill doesn't work as expected, you likely need to enter more values in the initial cells.

2. Select the cells that contain the initial values. Excel displays the Edit menu.

3. Tap Fill. Excel adds a Fill Down handle to the bottom edge of the selected range, and a Fill Right handle to the right edge of the selected range.

4. Tap and drag the Fill Down handle down to include the range you want to fill. When you release the handle, Excel fills the range with a series based on the initial values.

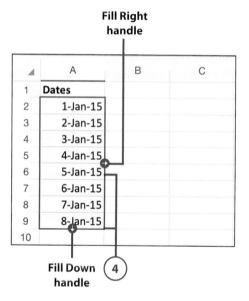

Filling Right

If you want to fill the value across columns, instead, tap and drag the Fill Right handle to the right to include the range you want to fill.

Copy a Range

The quickest way to become productive with Excel is to avoid reinventing your worksheets. If you have a formula that works, or a piece of formatting that you've put a lot of effort into, don't start from scratch if you need something similar. Instead, make a copy and then adjust the copy as necessary.

1. Select the range you want to copy. Excel displays the Edit menu.

2. Tap Copy.

3. Select the upper-left cell of the destination range.

4. Tap the cell again to display the Edit menu.

5. Tap Paste. Excel pastes a copy of the range to your destination.

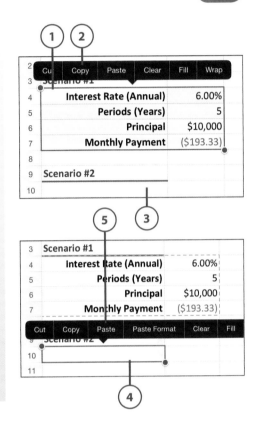

It's Not All Good

Don't Overwrite Existing Cells

Before copying a range to another area, look at the destination area and make sure you won't be overwriting any nonblank cells. Remember that you can tap Undo if you accidentally destroy some data. If you want to insert the range among some existing cells without overwriting existing data, see the "Insert a Range" section later in this chapter.

Move a Range

If a range is in the wrong section of a worksheet, you can move the range to the sheet area that you prefer.

1. Select the range you want to move. Excel displays the Edit menu.

2. Tap Cut.

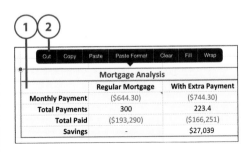

3. Select the upper-left cell of the destination range.

4. Tap the cell again to display the Edit menu.

5. Tap Paste. Excel pastes the range to the destination and deletes the original range data.

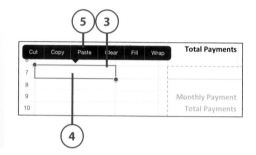

Insert a Range

When you begin a worksheet, you use up rows and columns sequentially as you add data and formulas. Invariably, however, you need to go back and add in some values or labels that you forgot or that you need for another part of the worksheet. When this happens, you need to insert ranges into your spreadsheet to make room for your new information.

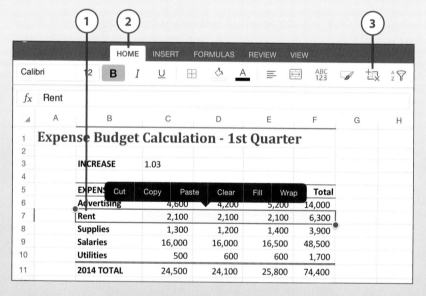

1. Select the range where you want the new range to appear. If you're inserting a horizontal range, select the cells above which you want the new range to appear. If you're inserting a vertical range, select the cells to the left of which you want the new range to appear.

2. Tap the Home tab.

3. Tap Insert & Delete Cells.

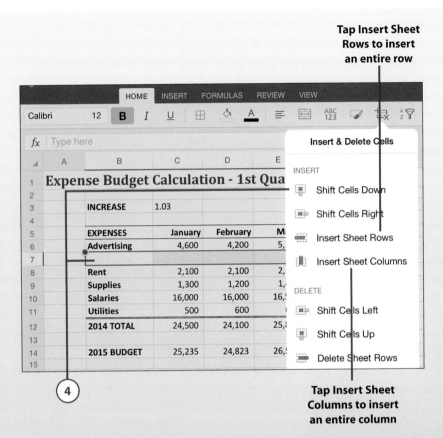

Tap Insert Sheet
Rows to insert
an entire row

Tap Insert Sheet
Columns to insert
an entire column

4. Tap the command that fits how you want Excel to adjust the existing cells to accommodate your inserted range. For example, if you're inserting a horizontal range, tap Shift Cells Down to make horizontal room for your new range. Similarly, if you're inserting a vertical range, tap Shift Cells Right to make vertical room for your new range.

Delete a Range

When you're building a worksheet, you often have to remove old or unnecessary data, and that requires you to delete ranges. It's often easiest to delete an entire row or column, but in some worksheets, you may need to delete only a single cell or a range of cells so as not to disturb the arrangement of surrounding data.

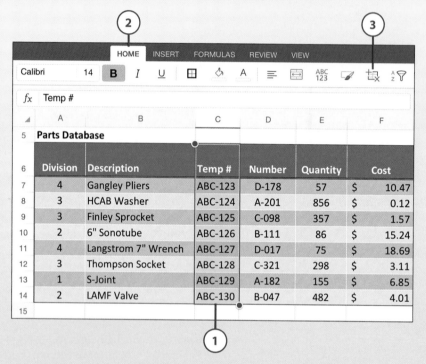

1. Select the range you want to delete.

2. Tap the Home tab.

3. Tap Insert & Delete Cells.

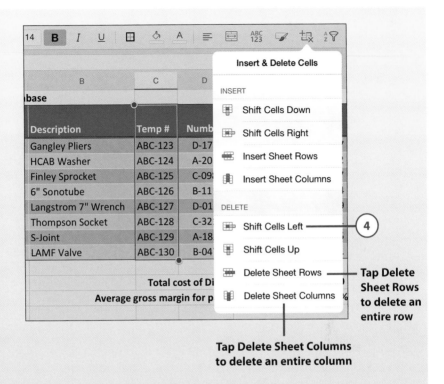

Tap Delete Sheet Rows to delete an entire row

Tap Delete Sheet Columns to delete an entire column

4. Tap the command that fits how you want Excel to adjust the existing cells to accommodate your deletion. For example, if you're deleting a horizontal range, tap Shift Cells Up to close up the horizontal gap that would otherwise appear in your range. Similarly, if you're deleting a vertical range, tap Shift Cells Left to close the vertical gap.

Formatting a Range

Your worksheets must produce the correct answers, of course, so most of your Excel time should be spent on getting your data and formulas entered accurately. However, you also need to spend time formatting your work, particularly if other people will be viewing or working with the spreadsheet. Labels, data, and formula results that have been augmented with fonts, borders, alignments, numeric formats, and other formatting are almost always easier to read and understand than unformatted sheets.

Learning About Data Formats

One of the best ways to improve the readability of a worksheet is to display data in a format that is logical, consistent, and straightforward. Formatting currency amounts with leading dollar signs, percentages with trailing percent signs, and large numbers with commas are a few of the ways you can improve your spreadsheet style.

When you enter numbers in a worksheet, Excel removes any leading or trailing zeros. For example, if you enter 0123.4500, Excel displays 123.45. The exception to this rule occurs when you enter a number that's wider than the cell. In this case, Excel usually expands the width of the column to fit the number. However, in some cases, Excel tailors the number to fit the cell by rounding off some decimal places. For example, the number 123.45678 might be displayed as 123.4568. Note that, in this case, the number is changed for display purposes only; Excel still retains the original number internally.

When you create a worksheet, each cell uses this format, known as the general number format, by default. If you want your numbers to appear differently, you can choose from among Excel's six categories of numeric formats:

- **Number**—The Number format has three components: the number of decimal places (0–30), whether the thousands separator (,) is used, and how negative numbers are displayed. For negative numbers, you can display the number with a leading minus sign, in red, surrounded by parentheses or in red surrounded by parentheses.

- **Currency**—The Currency format is similar to the Number format, except that the thousands separator is always used and the number appears with a leading dollar sign ($).

- **Accounting**—The Accounting format is the same as the Currency format, except Excel displays the dollar sign ($) flush left in the cell. All negative entries are displayed surrounded by parentheses.

- **Percentage**—The Percentage format displays the number multiplied by 100, with a percent sign (%) to the right of the number. For example, .506 is displayed as 50.6%. You can display 0–30 decimal places.

- **Fraction**—The Fraction format enables you to express decimal quantities as fractions.

- **Scientific**—The Scientific format displays the most significant number to the left of the decimal, 2–30 decimal places to the right of the decimal, and then the exponent. So, 123000 displays as 1.23E+05.

The quickest way to format numbers is to specify the format as you enter your data. For example, if you begin a dollar amount with a dollar sign ($), Excel automatically formats the number as currency. Similarly, if you type a percent sign (%) after a number, Excel automatically formats the number as percentage. Here are a few more examples of this technique. Note that you can enter a negative value using either the minus sign (–) or parentheses.

Number Entered	Number Displayed	Format Used
$1234.567	$1,234.57	Currency
($1234.5)	($1,234.50)	Currency
10%	10%	Percentage
123E+02	1.23E+04	Scientific
5 3/4	5 3/4	Fraction
0 3/4	3/4	Fraction
3/4	4-Mar	Date

Entering a Simple Fraction

Excel interprets a simple fraction such as 3/4 as a date (March 4, in this case). Always include a leading zero, followed by a space, if you want to enter a simple fraction from the Formula bar.

If you include dates or times in your worksheets, you need to make sure that they're presented in a readable, unambiguous format. For example, most people would interpret the date 8/5/14 as August 5, 2014. However, in some countries, this date would mean May 8, 2014. Similarly, if you use the time 2:45, do you mean a.m. or p.m.? To avoid these kinds of problems, you can use Excel's built-in date and time formats, listed in Table 7.1.

Table 7.1   Excel's Date and Time Formats

Format	Display
m/d	8/3
m/d/yy	8/3/14
mm/dd/yy	08/03/14
d-mmm	3-Aug
d-mmm-yy	3-Aug-14
dd-mmm-yy	03-Aug-14
mmm-yy	Aug-14
mmmm-yy	August-14
mmmm d, yyyy	August 3, 2014
h:mm AM/PM	3:10 PM
h:mm:ss AM/PM	3:10:45 PM
h:mm	15:10
h:mm:ss	15:10:45
mm:ss.0	10:45.7
[h]:mm:ss	27:10:45
m/d/yy h:mm AM/PM	8/23/14 3:10 PM
m/d/yy h:mm	8/23/14 15:10

You use the same methods to select date and time formats that you used for numeric formats. In particular, you can specify the date and time format as you input your data. For example, entering Jan-14 automatically formats the cell with the mmm-yy format. You also have the following commands available:

- **Date**—Choose this command to display a date using the mm/dd/yy format.

- **Time**—Choose this command to display a time using the hh:mm:ss AM/PM format.

Apply a Numeric or Date Format

Specifying the numeric format as you enter a number is fast and efficient because Excel guesses the format you want to use. Unfortunately, Excel sometimes guesses wrong (for example, interpreting a simple fraction as a date). In any case, you don't have access to all the available formats (for example, displaying negative dollar amounts in red). To overcome these limitations, you can select your numeric formats from a list.

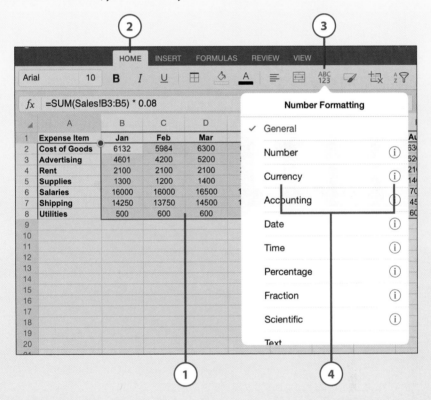

1. Select the cell or range of cells to which you want to apply the new format.

2. Tap the Home tab.

3. Tap Number Formatting. Excel displays its built-in formats.

4. If you want to use the default numeric format, tap the format name; otherwise, to specify options for the numeric format, tap the format's Info icon. Either way, Excel applies the default numeric format to the cell or range.

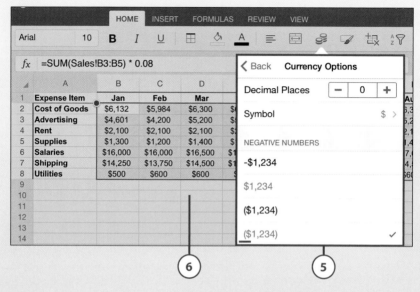

5. Select the format options you want to apply to your range. Excel applies the numeric format to the cell or range.

6. Tap outside the dialog to close it.

Customizing Numeric Formats

To get a bit more control over the numeric formats, drop down the Number Format list and then tap More Number Formats. The Number tab of the Format Cells dialog box enables you to specify the number of decimal places, the currency symbol, and more.

Control the Number of Decimal Places

You can make your numeric values easier to read and interpret by adjusting the number of decimal places that Excel displays. For example, you might want to ensure that all dollar-and-cent values show two decimal places, while dollar-only values show no decimal places. You can either decrease or increase the number of decimal places that Excel displays.

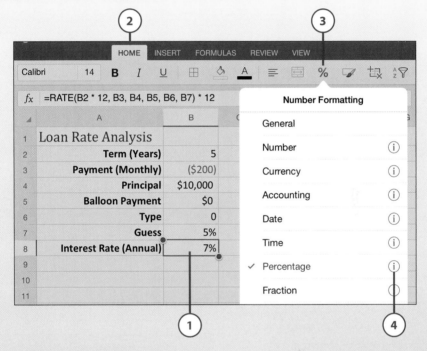

1. Select the range you want to format.
2. Tap the Home tab.
3. Tap Number Formatting.
4. Tap the Info icon beside the currently applied numeric format.

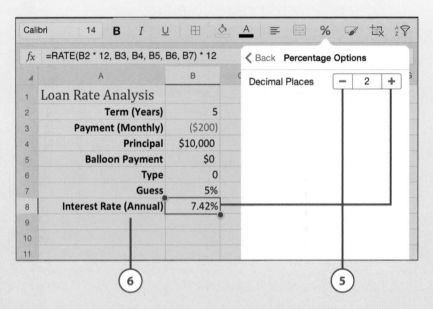

5. Tap the + or – button to set the number of decimal places you want to display.

6. Tap outside the dialog to close it.

Resize a Column

The AutoFit feature resizes a column's width to improve the appearance of your worksheet in a number of different ways. For example, if you're faced with a truncated text entry or a number that Excel shows as ######, AutoFit will enlarge the column so the entry can appear in full. In general, AutoFit adjusts the column's width to fit the widest item in the column.

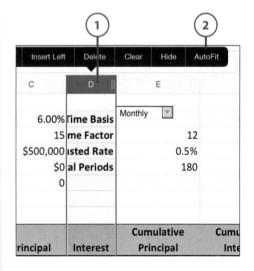

1. Tap the header of the column you want to resize. Excel displays the column's Edit menu.

2. Tap AutoFit. Excel sets the column width and returns you to the worksheet.

Resizing a Column with Gestures

You can also resize a column using gestures. For example, you can tap and drag the right edge of the column header: Either drag the edge of the column header to the right (to increase the width) or left (to decrease the width). You can also double-tap the right edge of the column header to automatically size the column to its widest entry.

Resize Rows

Although Excel normally adjusts row heights automatically to accommodate the tallest font in a row, it doesn't always do this. In that case, you can use AutoFit to adjust the height to fit the tallest item in the row.

1. Tap the header of the row you want to resize. Excel displays the row's Edit menu.

2. Tap AutoFit. Excel sets the row height and returns you to the worksheet.

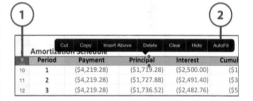

Resizing a Row with Gestures

You can also use touchscreen gestures to resize a row. For example, you can tap and drag the bottom edge of the row header: Either drag the edge of the row header down (to increase the height) or up (to decrease the height). You can also double-tap the bottom edge of the row header to automatically size the row to its tallest entry.

Add Borders

Excel lets you place borders around your worksheet cells or ranges. This is useful for enclosing different parts of the worksheet, defining data entry areas, and separating headings from data. You can also use borders to make a range easier to read. For example, if a range has totals on the bottom row, you can add a border above the totals.

1. Select the range you want to format.

2. Tap the Home tab.

3. Tap Cell Borders. Excel displays a list of border types.

4. Tap the border type you want to use. Excel applies the border to the range. Repeat as necessary.

5. Tap outside the list to close it.

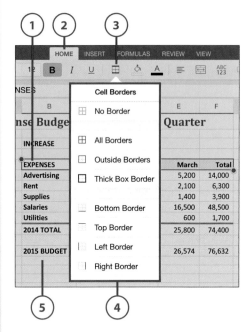

Wrap Text Within a Cell

If you type more text in a cell than can fit horizontally, Excel either displays the text over the next cell if that cell is empty or displays only part of the text if the next cell contains data. To prevent Excel from showing only truncated cell data, you can format the cell to wrap text within the cell. Excel then increases the height of the row to ensure that all the text displays.

1. Select the range you want to format. The range Edit menu appears.

2. Tap Wrap. Excel wraps the text as needed within each cell in the range and then increases the height of the row to ensure that all the text displays.

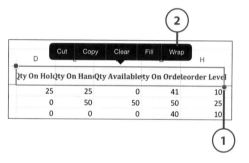

Chart area   Data series   Chart title   Gridlines   Plot area

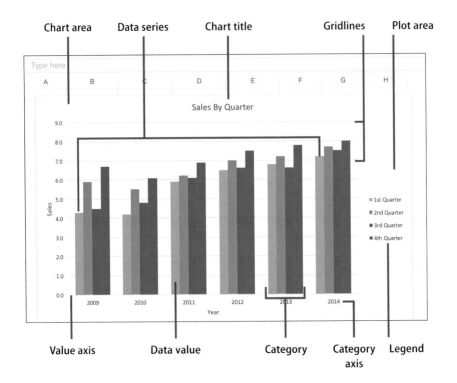

Value axis   Data value   Category   Category axis   Legend

In this chapter, you learn about creating, customizing, and formatting charts to help visualize your Excel data.

→ Converting Excel data into a chart
→ Working with Excel's different chart types
→ Moving and resizing a chart
→ Applying chart styles and colors
→ Adding chart titles, a legend, and data labels
→ Changing the layout of a chart

Visualizing Excel Data with Charts

One of the best ways to analyze your worksheet data—or get your point across to other people—is to display your data visually in a chart. Excel gives you tremendous flexibility when creating charts: It enables you to place charts in separate documents or directly on the worksheet itself. Not only that, but you have dozens of different chart formats to choose from, and if none of Excel's built-in formats is just right, you can further customize these charts to suit your needs.

Creating a Chart

When plotting your worksheet data, you have two basic options: You can create an embedded chart that sits on top of your worksheet and can be moved, sized, and formatted; or you can create a separate chart sheet. Whether you choose to embed your charts or store them in separate sheets, the charts are linked with the worksheet data. Any changes you make to the data are automatically updated in the chart.

Before getting to the specifics of creating a chart, you should familiarize your-self with some basic chart terminology:

- **Category**—A grouping of data values on the category horizontal axis.

- **Category axis**—The axis (usually the x-axis) that contains the category groupings.

- **Chart area**—The area on which the chart is drawn.

- **Data marker**—A symbol that represents a specific data value. The sym-bol used depends on the chart type. In a column chart, for example, each column is a marker.

- **Data series**—A collection of related data values. Normally, the marker for each value in a series has the same pattern.

- **Data value**—A single piece of data. Also called a *data point.*

- **Gridlines**—Optional horizontal and vertical extensions of the axis tick marks. These make data values easier to read.

- **Legend**—A guide that shows the colors, patterns, and symbols used by the markers for each data series.

- **Plot area**—The area bounded by the category and value axes. It contains the data points and gridlines.

- **Tick mark**—A small line that intersects the category axis or the value axis. It marks divisions in the chart's categories or scales.

- **Value axis**—The axis (usually the y-axis) that contains the data values.

Create a Chart

Creating a chart in Excel involves selecting the data you want to visualize and then choosing the chart type that best displays that data.

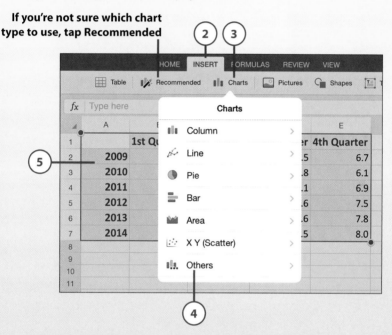

If you're not sure which chart type to use, tap Recommended

1. Select the range you want to plot, including the row and column labels if there are any. Make sure that no blank rows are between the column labels and the data.

2. Tap Insert.

3. Tap Charts. Excel displays a gallery of chart types.

4. Tap a chart type. Excel displays a gallery of chart subtypes.

Using a Recommended Chart Type

It's not always easy to know in advance what chart type will best display your data. Instead of guessing, you can let Excel help by tapping the Recommended command. Given the structure and type of the worksheet data you select, Excel displays a few chart types it deems best.

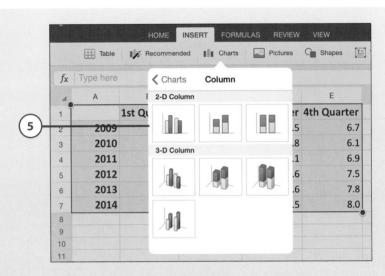

5. Tap a chart subtype. Excel inserts the chart.

Working with Charts

After you create a chart, Excel offers various tools for working with it, including changing the chart type, moving and resizing the chart, and changing its layout. The next few sections provide the details.

Understanding Excel's Chart Types

To help you choose the chart type that best presents your data, the following list provides brief descriptions of all Excel's chart types:

- **Area chart**—An *area chart* shows the relative contributions over time that each data series makes to the whole picture. The smaller the area a data series takes up, the smaller its contribution to the whole.

- **Bar chart**—A *bar chart* compares distinct items or shows single items at distinct intervals. A bar chart is laid out with categories along the vertical axis and values along the horizontal axis. This format lends itself to competitive comparisons because categories appear to be "ahead" or "behind."

- **Column chart**—Like a bar chart, a *column chart* compares distinct items or shows single items at distinct intervals. However, a column chart is laid out with categories along the horizontal axis and values along the vertical axis (as are most Excel charts). This format is best suited for comparing items over time. Excel offers various column chart formats, including *stacked columns*. A stacked column chart is similar to an area chart; series values are stacked on top of each other to show the relative contributions of each series. Although an area chart is useful for showing the flow of the relative contributions over time, a stacked column chart is better for showing the contributions at discrete intervals.

- **Line chart**—A *line chart* shows how a data series changes over time. The category (x) axis usually represents a progression of even increments (such as days or months), and the series points are plotted on the value (y) axis. Excel offers several stock chart formats, including an Open, High, Low, Close chart (also called a *candlestick chart*), which is useful for plotting stock-market prices.

- **Pie chart**—A *pie chart* shows the proportion of the whole that is contributed by each value in a single data series. The whole is represented as a circle (the "pie"), and each value is displayed as a proportional "slice" of the circle.

- **XY (scatter) chart**—An *XY chart* (also called a scatter chart) shows the relationship between numeric values in two different data series. It also can plot a series of data pairs in an x,y coordinate. An XY chart is a variation of the line chart in which the category axis is replaced by a second value axis. You can use XY charts for plotting items such as survey data, mathematical functions, and experimental results.

- **Stock chart**—A *stock chart* is optimized for displaying stock data, including opening, closing, high, and low prices, as well as stock trading volume.

- **Surface chart**—You can use a *surface chart* to analyze two sets of data and determine the optimum combination of the two. A surface chart is like a topographical map.

- **Radar chart**—A *radar chart* makes comparisons within a data series and between data series relative to a center point. Each category is shown with a value axis extending from the center point. To understand this concept, think of a radar screen in an airport control tower. The tower itself is the central point, and the radar radiates a beam (a value axis). When the radar makes contact with a plane, a blip appears onscreen. In a radar chart, this data point is shown with a data marker.

Change the Chart Type

If you feel that the current chart type is not showing your data in the best way, you can change the chart type. This enables you to experiment not only with the nine different chart types offered by Excel, but also with its 50 chart subtypes.

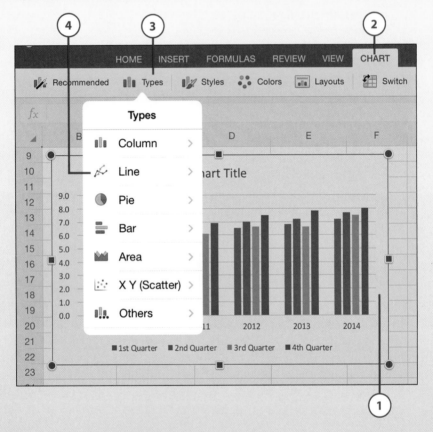

1. Tap the chart to select it.
2. Tap the Chart tab.
3. Tap Types. The Types popover appears.
4. Tap a chart type. Excel displays a gallery of chart subtypes.

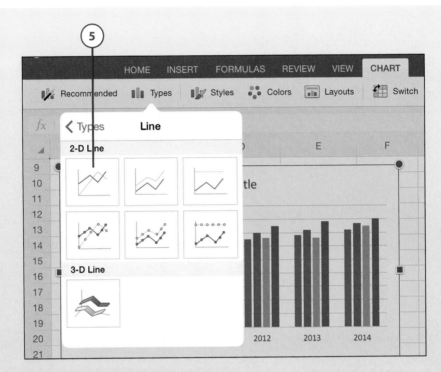

5. Tap a chart subtype. Excel updates the chart.

Move a Chart

You can move a chart to another part of the worksheet. This is useful if the chart is blocking the worksheet data or if you want the chart to appear in a particular part of the worksheet.

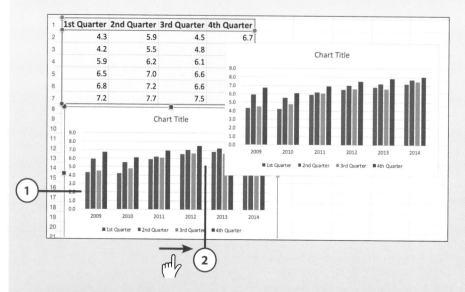

1. Tap the chart to select it.

2. Tap and drag an empty section of the chart to the location you want. As you drag, Excel moves the chart.

Dragging the Chart

You can drag any part of the chart to move it. However, avoid dragging any of the selection handles (see the next section), or you'll just resize the chart.

Resize a Chart

You can resize a chart. For example, if you find that the chart is difficult to read, making the chart bigger often solves the problem. Similarly, if the chart takes up too much space on the worksheet, you can make it smaller.

Selection handles

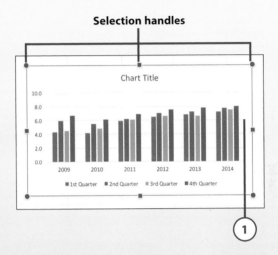

1. Tap the chart. Excel displays a border around the chart, which includes selection handles on the corners and sides.

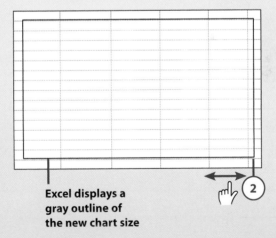

**Excel displays a
gray outline of
the new chart size**

2. Tap and drag a selection handle until the chart is the size you want. When you release the screen, Excel resizes the chart.

Apply a Chart Style

You can quickly format your chart by applying a chart style, which governs the formatting applied to the chart background, data markers, gridlines, and more.

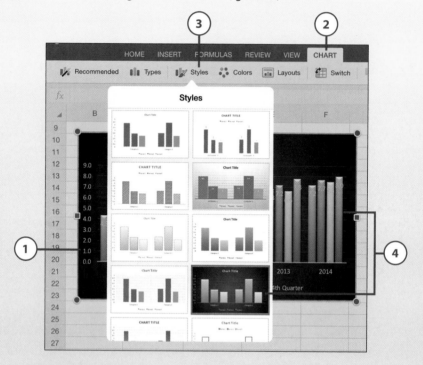

1. Tap the chart.

2. Tap the Chart tab.

3. Tap Style. Excel displays the Styles gallery.

4. Tap the style you want to apply.

Modify the Chart Colors

If you want a different look for your chart data markers, you can apply one of Excel's pre-defined color schemes.

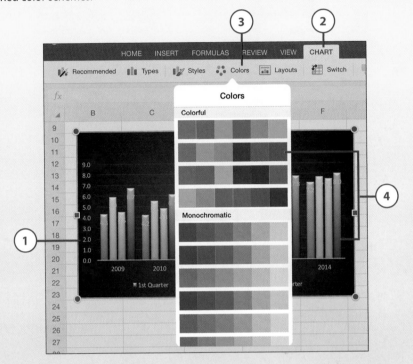

1. Tap the chart.

2. Tap the Chart tab.

3. Tap Colors. Excel displays the Colors gallery.

4. Tap the color scheme you want to apply.

Switch the Chart Layout

You can quickly format your chart by applying a different chart layout. The chart layout includes elements such as the titles, data labels, legend, and gridlines. The Layouts feature in Excel enables you to apply these elements in different combinations in just a few steps.

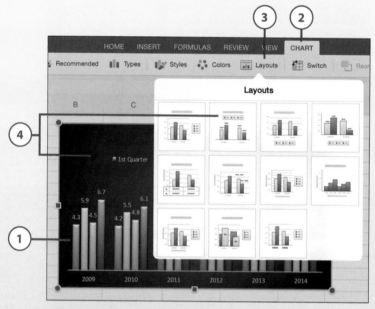

1. Tap the chart.
2. Tap the Chart tab.
3. Tap Colors. Excel displays the Layouts gallery.
4. Tap the layout you want to apply.

Data Table

One of the chart layouts includes a data table, which is a rectangular grid that shows the data series, categories, and values. This makes it easy to reference specific chart values if the original worksheet data isn't visible.

Add new
slides

Insert a
table

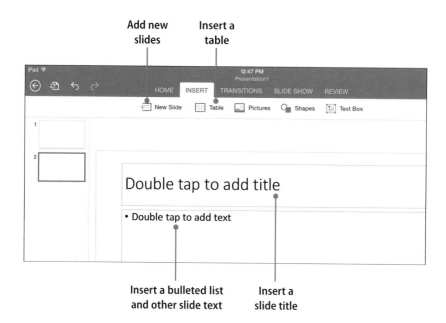

Insert a bulleted list
and other slide text

Insert a
slide title

In this chapter, you learn the basics of building a PowerPoint presentation, from inserting slides to adding text, graphics, charts, and other content.

→ Understanding slide layouts
→ Inserting and duplicating slides
→ Adding slide content, such as text, bulleted lists, and tables
→ Rearranging and hiding slides
→ Adding presentation notes to a slide

Building a PowerPoint Presentation

It's probably not a stretch to claim that, in terms of market share, PowerPoint is the most dominant software program in the world. A few years ago, Microsoft said that PowerPoint had 95% of the presentation graphics market, but it wouldn't surprise me if that number were even higher today. With many of our kids learning and using PowerPoint in school, and with an eminently usable iPad version of PowerPoint now available, this dominance is poised to continue into the foreseeable future.

In short, we live in a PowerPoint world.

So learning how to get along in this world is important, and this is what the next two chapters are all about. The focus is on a PowerPoint "middle way" that avoids the two most common PowerPoint faults: drab, lifeless presentations that are ineffective because they bore the audience to tears, and "PowerPointlessness"—those overly fancy formats, transitions, sounds, and other effects that have no discernible purpose, use, or benefit. With the middle way, you learn how to create attractive presentations that offer visual interest without sacrificing clarity.

Adding a Slide to the Presentation

The heart and soul of any presentation is the collection of slides that comprise the bulk of its content and that serve as both the focal point and the organizing structure of the speech. The slides are the bridge between the audience and the speaker. Building an effective presentation consists mostly of creating and organizing slides, which in turn involves four things:

- The content—the text and graphics—presented on each slide

- The organization of the content presented on each slide

- The formatting applied to each slide: fonts, colors, background, and so on

- The placement of the slides within the context of the entire presentation

The bulk of this chapter takes you through various PowerPoint techniques that support these four design ideas.

Understanding Slide Layouts

Before we get to the specifics of adding a slide, you should understand that all slides contain some combination of the following three elements:

- **Title**—This is a text box that you normally use to add a title for the slide.

- **Text**—This is a text box that you normally use to add text to the slide, which is usually a collection of bullets.

- **Content**—This is a container into which you add any type of content supported by PowerPoint: text, pictures, or a SmartArt graphic. In some cases, PowerPoint displays placeholders for specific types of content. For example, a Picture placeholder can contain only a picture.

In each case, the new slide contains one or more placeholders, and your job is to fill in a placeholder with text or a content object. Each slide uses some combination of Title, Text, and Content placeholders, and the arrangement of these placeholders on a slide is called the slide layout. PowerPoint for iPad offers eleven layouts:

- **Title Slide**—A slide with two text boxes: a larger one for the overall presentation title and a smaller one for the subtitle.

- **Title and Content**—A slide with a Title placeholder and a Content placeholder.

- **Section Header**—A slide with two Text placeholders: one for the description and one for the title of a new presentation section.

- **Two Content**—A slide with a Title placeholder above two Content placeholders placed side by side.

- **Comparison**—A slide with a Title placeholder, two Content placeholders placed side by side, and two Text placeholders (one above each Content placeholder).

- **Title Only**—A slide with just a Title placeholder.

- **Blank**—A slide with no placeholders.

- **Content with Caption**—A Content placeholder with two Text placeholders to the left of it: one for the content title and the other for the content description.

- **Picture with Caption**—A Picture placeholder with two Text placeholders beneath it: one for the picture title and the other for the picture description.

- **Title and Vertical Text**—A Title placeholder with a Text placeholder beneath it that has been configured to display text vertically rather than horizontally, which is useful if you have a lot of text to enter. (Rotate the iPad into portrait position to read the text.)

- **Vertical Title and Text**—A Title placeholder on the right, with a Text placeholder to the left, both of which have been configured to display text vertically rather than horizontally. (Rotate the iPad into portrait position to read the text.)

Insert a New Slide

Inserting a new slide into your presentation is a straightforward matter of deciding what content you want on the slide and then deciding which slide layout would best display that content.

1. In the slide sorter, tap the slide after which you want the new slide to appear.

2. Tap the Insert tab.

3. Tap New Slide.

4. Tap the slide layout you want to use. PowerPoint inserts the new slide.

Duplicate a Slide

If you have a slide in the current presentation that has similar content and formatting to what you want for a new slide, you can save yourself a great deal of time by inserting a duplicate of that slide and then adjusting the copy as needed.

1. In the slide sorter, tap and hold the slide you want to duplicate until the menu appears.

2. Tap Duplicate. PowerPoint creates a copy of the slide and inserts the copy below the selected slide.

Duplicating via Copy-and-Paste

For a bit more control over where the duplicate appears, tap and hold the original slide until the menu appears; then tap Copy. Select the slide after which you want the copy to appear and then tap Paste.

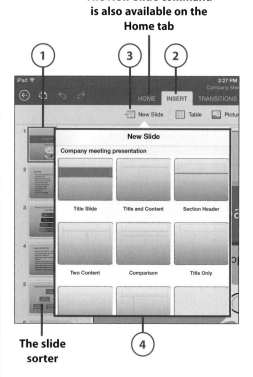

The New Slide command is also available on the Home tab

The slide sorter

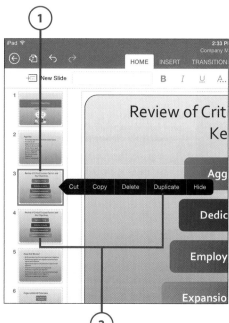

Adding Data to a Slide

After you have added one or more slides, the next step is to fill in the placeholders. The next few sections take you through some of the details; although I ignore the picture-related icons because I already covered adding graphics in Chapter 3, "Working with Office for iPad Graphics."

Adding Text

With a Title or Text placeholder, double-tap inside the placeholder to enable editing, and then type your text. In a Text placeholder, PowerPoint assumes that you'll be adding bullet points, so the Bullets format is on by default. PowerPoint supports four standard list levels, which determine where a bullet appears in the list hierarchy:

- **Level 1**—This is the main level. It uses a solid, round bullet and appears flush with the left side of the placeholder.

- **Level 2**—This is the next level in the hierarchy. It uses a slightly smaller bullet and appears indented by one tab stop from the left side of the placeholder.

- **Level 3**—This is the next level in the hierarchy. It uses an even smaller bullet and appears indented by two tab stops from the left side of the placeholder.

- **Level 4**—This is the final level in the hierarchy. It uses the smallest bullet and appears indented by three tab stops from the left side of the placeholder.

You can actually create higher and higher levels, but the bullet remains the same size and PowerPoint simply indents the bullets further from the left. The next section illustrates what some of these levels look like.

Create a Bulleted List

Populating a Text placeholder with a bulleted list will likely be your most common PowerPoint chore.

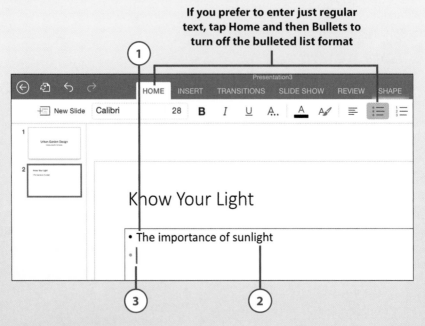

If you prefer to enter just regular text, tap Home and then Bullets to turn off the bulleted list format

Know Your Light

• The importance of sunlight

1. Tap inside a Text placeholder to open it for editing. PowerPoint displays the first bullet.

2. Type the text for the list item.

3. Press Enter. PowerPoint adds a bullet for the next item in the list.

4. Repeat steps 2 and 3 to add more items to the list.

5. To increase the list level of the current item, tap the Home tab and then tap Increase List Level.

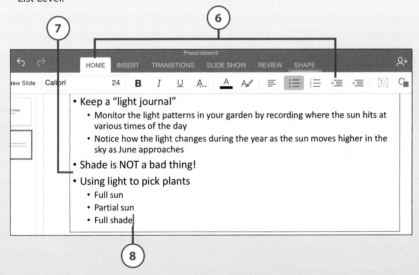

6. To decrease the list level of the current item, tap the Home tab and then tap Decrease List Level.

7. Repeat steps 2–6 until your list is complete.

8. Position the insertion point at the end of the last item, and then press Enter twice to tell PowerPoint that your bulleted list is done.

Inserting a Tab

You can also increase the list level by inserting a tab. Tap and hold for a few seconds at the beginning of the item you want to modify. In the menu that appears, tap Insert and then tap Tab.

>>>Go Further
CONVERTING REGULAR TEXT TO A BULLETED LIST

What if a slide already includes regular text that you'd prefer to display as a bulleted list? Select the entire list, tap the Home tab, tap the Bullets icon on the Ribbon, and then tap the bullet style you want to use. PowerPoint converts the text into a bulleted list.

Add a Table

If you want to present data that would look best in a row-and-column format, use a table. Note that a PowerPoint table is nearly identical to a Word table, so see the section "Building a Table" in Chapter 5, "Working with Page Layout and Design in Word," for more table details.

1. Select a slide that contains a Content placeholder.

2. Tap the Content placeholder.

3. Tap the Insert tab.

4. Tap Table. PowerPoint inserts an empty table into the slide.

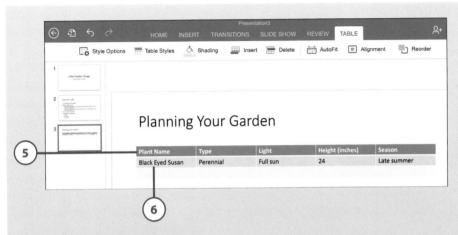

5. Type your column headings.

6. Type your table data.

Working with Slides

Now that your presentation is populated with a few content filled slides, it's time to learn a few useful techniques for working with them. The rest of this chapter shows you how to rearrange slides, hide a slide, and add slide notes.

Rearrange Slides

If you have one or more slides that don't appear in the correct position within your presentation, you can move them to the correct positions.

1. In the slide sorter, tap and hold for a few seconds on the slide you want to move.

2. Tap Cut.

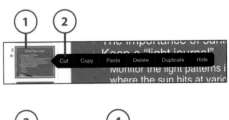

3. Tap and hold for a few seconds on the slide after which you want the moved slide to appear.

4. Tap Paste. PowerPoint moves the slide into the new position.

Hide a Slide

In some presentations, there may be slides you don't want to show:

- You might have a short version and a long version of a presentation.

- You might want to omit certain slides, depending on whether you are presenting to managers, salespeople, or engineers.

- You might have "internal" and "external" versions; that is, you might have one version for people who work at your company and a different version for people from outside the company.

You could accommodate these different scenarios by creating copies of a presentation and then removing slides as appropriate. However, this process takes a great deal of work, wastes disk space, and is inefficient when one slide changes and you have to make the same change in every version of the presentation that includes the slide.

A much better solution is to use a single presentation but mark the slides you don't want to show as hidden. PowerPoint skips hidden slides when you present the show.

1. In the slide sorter, tap and hold for a few seconds on the slide you want to hide.

2. Tap Hide. PowerPoint displays a faded version of the slide thumbnail and adds a universal "Not" symbol to the upper-left corner of the slide thumbnail.

Unhiding a Slide

To unhide a slide, tap and hold for a few seconds on the slide thumbnail; then tap Unhide.

Deleting a Slide

If you have a slide that you no longer need, you should delete it to reduce the size of the presentation, reduce clutter in the slide sorter, and prevent the slide from appearing when you present the project. To delete a slide, use the slide sorter to tap and hold for a few seconds on the slide you want to remove; then tap Delete.

Add Notes to a Slide

When determining the content of a presentation, you keep the actual amount of information on a slide to a minimum—just the high-level points to provide the framework for the topics you want to present. How, then, do you keep track of the details you want to cover for each slide? You add notes to the presentation. When you run through the presentation on another computer (you can't view notes on the iPad), PowerPoint's Reading View mode enables you to display the notes.

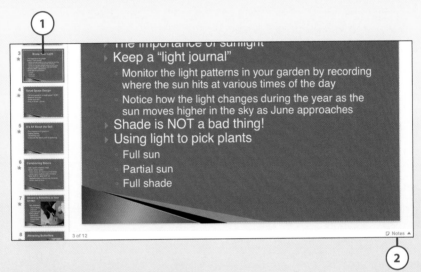

1. Tap the slide you want to work with.

2. Tap Notes. PowerPoint opens the Notes box.

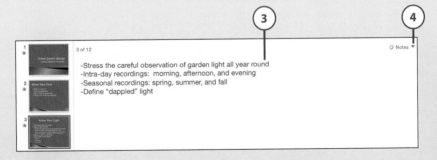

3. Type your notes.

4. Tap Notes to close the Notes box.

>>>*Go Further*
USING SLIDE NOTES

Here are some suggested ways you can use notes:

- As additional details for the audience.

- As a student guide. If you use a presentation as your primary teaching medium, you can put additional information on notes pages for your learners.

- As an instructor's guide. Again, if you teach from your presentation, you might have points you want to make, or other information associated with a particular slide. Add this information as notes, and you have your instructor's guide, perfectly in sync with the information you're giving your learners.

- As your presentation notes.

- As additional detailed handouts for your audience.

The first two points here apply to both offline presentations (where you present in front of an audience) and online presentations (where audience members run the show themselves), but the last three apply only to offline presentations.

Add transitions between sides   Set transition effect options   Start the slide show

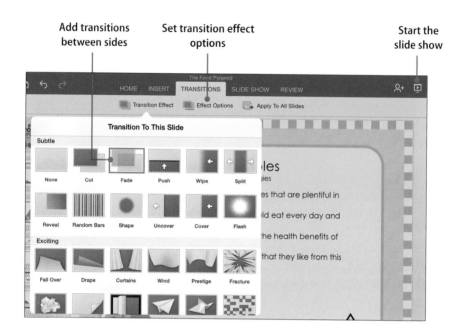

In this chapter, you learn how to work with PowerPoint slide shows, including how to set up slide animations, work out slide timings, record narration, and run the slide show.

→ Adding transitions to your slides
→ Working transition options
→ Starting and navigating a slide show
→ Annotating a running slide show

10

Working with PowerPoint Slide Shows

In Chapter 9, "Building a PowerPoint Presentation," I mentioned that your goal when creating your slides should be to achieve a balance between eye candy and content. That is, although you need to tweak your slide fonts, colors, and effects to a certain extent to add visual interest, you do not want to go so far that your message is lost.

The same idea applies to the slide show as a whole, particularly if you want to add some dynamism to the presentation with slide transitions. These are fine additions to any presentation, but going overboard and overwhelming your audience is easy to do. This chapter gives you the details and techniques that can help you create the dynamic and interesting slide shows that audiences crave.

Defining Slide Transitions

Many years ago, someone defined *fritterware* as any software program that offered so many options and settings, you could fritter away hours at a time tweaking and playing with the program. That description certainly applies to the desktop version of PowerPoint, because wasting away entire afternoons playing with transitions, entrance effects, motion paths, and other animation features is not hard. However, PowerPoint for iPad implements only a sub-set of these features—specifically, just transitions—so it's less likely to have adverse effects on your productivity.

Transition Guidelines

Before you learn how to apply slide transitions, it's worth taking a bit of time now to run through a few guidelines for making the best use of these slide show animations:

- **Enhance your content**—The goal of any animation should always be to enhance your presentation, either to emphasize a slide object or to keep up your audience's interest. Resist the temptation to add effects just because you think they are cool or fun because chances are most of your audience won't see them that way.

- **Remember that transitions can be useful**—Using some sort of effect to transition from one slide to the next is a good idea because it adds visual interest, gives the audience a short breather, and helps you control the pacing of your presentation.

- **Remember that transitions can be distracting**—A slide transition is only as useful as it is unremarkable. If everybody leaves your presenta-tion thinking "Nice transitions!", then you have a problem because they *should* be thinking about your message. Simple transitions such as fades, wipes, and dissolves add interest but do not get in the way. However, if you have objects flying in from all corners of the screen, your content will seem like a letdown.

- **For transitions, variety is *not* the spice of life**—Avoid the temptation to use many different transitions in a single presentation. Just as slide text looks awful if you use too many fonts, your presentations will look amateurish if you use too many animated effects.

- **Match your transitions to your audience**—If you are presenting to sales and marketing types, your entire presentation will be a bit on the flashy side, so you can probably get away with more elaborate effects. In a no-nonsense presentation to board members, transitions should be as simple as possible.

Set Up a Slide Transition

A slide transition is a special effect that displays the next slide in the presentation. For example, in a fade transition, the next slide gradually materializes, whereas in a blinds transition the next slide appears with an effect similar to opening Venetian blinds. PowerPoint for iPad has 45 different slide transitions.

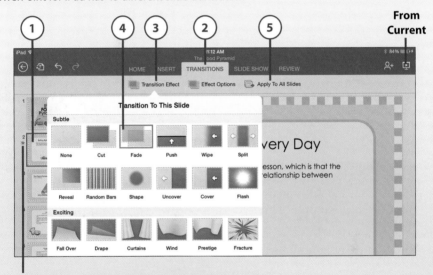

PowerPoint indicates that a slide has a transition by adding a star icon with "speed lines"

1. Tap the slide you want to work with.
2. Tap the Transitions tab.
3. Tap Transition Effect. PowerPoint displays a gallery of transitions.
4. Tap the transition effect you want.
5. If you want to apply the transition to every slide in the presentation, tap Apply To All Slides.

>>>Go Further
PREVIEWING THE TRANSITION

Unfortunately, PowerPoint for iPad doesn't preview the transition when you select it, nor does it offer a Preview command. The easiest way to get a quick preview of the current slide's transition is to tap the From Current icon that appears on the far right of the Ribbon. This command launches the slide show from the current slide but for our purposes here it first displays the slide's transition effect. To return to the slide, swipe down on the screen and then tap End Slide Show.

Set Transition Effect Options

PowerPoint for iPad offers only a limited set of options for customizing transition effects. The options vary depending on the effect, but in most cases you can set only the direction of the transition.

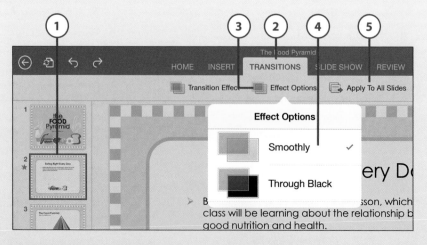

1. Tap the slide that has the transition you want to customize.

2. Tap the Transitions tab.

3. Tap Effect Options. PowerPoint displays a gallery of options for the effect.

4. Tap the transition effect option you want to apply.

5. If you want to apply both the transition effect and the option to every slide in the presentation, tap Apply To All Slides.

Effects Without Options

Although most transition effects come with options, some do not. Therefore, if you find that the Effect Options command is disabled after you choose a transition effect, it means that effect doesn't have any options to set.

It's Not All Good

Applying the Option to All Slides

PowerPoint for iPad's Apply To All Slides command is a blunt instrument. Ideally, it would apply your transition effect option only to those slides in the presentation that use the same effect as the one used by the current slide. That's not the case, however. When you tap Apply To All Slides, PowerPoint for iPad updates *every* slide in the presentation with both the current slide's transition effect and the effect option you selected. This applies even to slides that you previously configured with a different transition, so wield the Apply To All Slides command with care.

Running a Slide Show

With your slides laid out, the text perfected, the formatting just right, and your transitions in place, you're now ready to present your slide show. The next few sections show you how to start and navigate a slide show, as well as how to annotate a running slide show.

Start the Slide Show from the Beginning

In most cases, you'll want to start the slide show from the beginning.

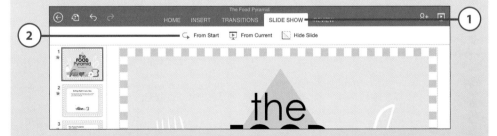

1. Tap the Slide Show tab.

2. Tap From Start. PowerPoint starts the slide show and displays the first slide.

Start the Slide Show from a Specific Slide

If there's a particular place within the slide show that you prefer to start, you can tell PowerPoint to begin the show from that slide.

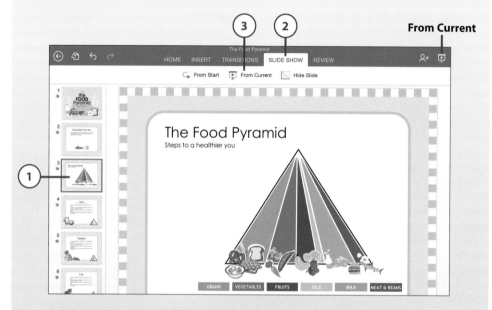

1. Tap the slide that you want to use as the starting point for the slide show.

2. Tap the Slide Show tab.

3. Tap From Current. PowerPoint starts the slide show and displays the current slide.

Shortcut

You can also start your slide show from the current slide by tapping the From Current icon that appears on the far right of the PowerPoint for iPad Ribbon.

Navigate Slides

With your slide show running, you now need to navigate from one slide to the next and then end the slide show when you're done.

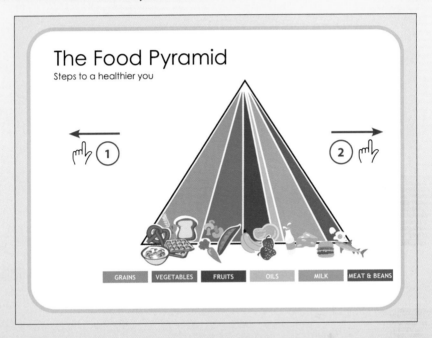

1. Swipe the screen from right to left. PowerPoint displays the next slide.

2. To return to the previous slide, swipe left to right.

Displaying Animations

If the presentation was created in the desktop version of PowerPoint, it might have animations applied to the slide objects. In that case, swiping left will run the next animation in the current slide.

3. To end the slide show before the last slide, swipe down on the screen. PowerPoint displays the slide show controls.

4. Tap End Slide Show.

Using the Laser Pointer

You can "point" to a slide object during the presentation by letting your finger rest lightly on the screen. PowerPoint adds a laser pointer under your fingertip, and you then slide your finger along the screen to move the pointer.

Ending the Slide Show "Naturally"

When you swipe left on the last slide, PowerPoint displays the message "End of slide show. Swipe forward to exit." This means that you need to swipe right to left to exit. You can also return to the last slide by swiping left to right.

Annotate a Slide Show

If you want to make handwritten (or more accurately, finger-written) notes on a slide, or if you want to highlight key bits of text during a presentation, you can annotate a slide. You can select either a pen to write words or draw shapes such as arrows or a highlighter to emphasize text passages with a color.

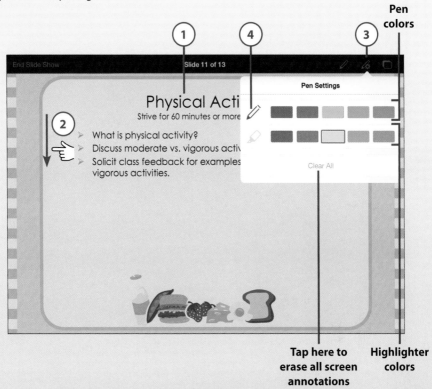

1. During a slide show, display the slide you want to annotate.

2. Swipe down on the screen. PowerPoint displays the slide show controls.

3. Tap Pen Settings.

4. Tap either a pen color or a highlighter color.

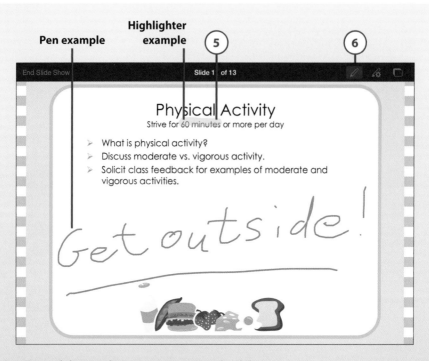

5. Tap and drag on the screen to annotate the slide.

6. When you're done, tap Pen to turn off the annotating.

Clearing Annotations

If your annotations don't turn out quite right, you can start over by tapping Pen Settings and then tapping Clear All.

It's Not All Good

Annotations Are Not Saved!

When you annotate your slide show, bear in mind that your efforts are merely temporary. That is, unlike the desktop version of PowerPoint, PowerPoint for iPad does *not* ask if you want to save your annotations when you exit the slide show. In fact, as soon as you move to a different slide in the current slide show, PowerPoint for iPad erases all annotations you added to the previous slide.

Insert text   Add sections   Add pages   Tag items

Create a
to-do list

In this chapter, you learn about building a OneNote notebook, working with sections and pages, entering text, tables, and lists, and tagging items.

→ Building a notebook by adding sections and pages

→ Color-coding pages

→ Entering text and working with page containers

→ Tagging items on a page

→ Building OneNote tables and to-do lists

Building a OneNote Notebook

The Office for iPad applications that you've learned about so far in the book—Word, Excel, and PowerPoint—enable you to enter data in a relatively structured format: Word with its sentences and paragraphs; Excel with its rows, columns, and cells; and PowerPoint with its slides and slide placeholders. However, the data we deal with in our lives isn't always so structured: thoughts, ideas, inspirations, to-do lists, phone numbers, names of books to read and movies to see, website and email addresses, and on and on.

Many of us keep notebooks handy for jotting down these random bits of data, but we live in an electronic age, so wouldn't it be great to jot down stray bits of information in a digital format?

I'm happy to report that the answer to that question is, "You can!" The electronic version of your paper notebook is OneNote, which enables you to quickly and easily record just about anything that you'd normally scribble on a piece of paper. With OneNote, you can do all that and also much more:

- Paste pictures, clip art, and text

- Insert links to websites

- Organize data into tables

- Share your notes with other people

Working with Sections

In the real world, a notebook might come with (or you might add) several tabs that divide the notebook into separate sections, each with its own collection of pages. This is the metaphor that OneNote uses. OneNote files are called notebooks, and each notebook consists of a series of sections, and each section consists of one or more pages. You use these pages to enter your free-form notes and other data.

A notebook is a collection of different types of data scraps from a variety of sources. It's important to impose some kind of order on all those scraps so that the notebook doesn't devolve into an unruly mess where it takes too long to find what you need.

Within each notebook, the main level of organization is the section, which is represented by a tab in the left pane of the notebook. You use the sections to break down the notebook's overall topic or theme into smaller subjects. You can create as many sections as you need because there's no practical limit on the number of sections you can add to a notebook.

OneNote is a hierarchical storage system, with notebooks at the top level, sections at the second level, and pages at the third level. You can fine-tune this hierarchy by taking advantage of OneNote's color-coding features, which enable you to link similar items visually by applying the same color to those items.

Insert a New Section

When you create a new notebook using OneNote, the resulting file has a single section that contains a single page. However, you are free to add more sections as needed.

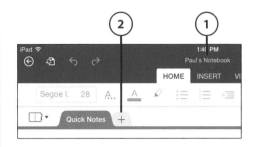

1. Open the notebook you want to work with.

2. Tap the Create a New Section icon. OneNote creates the new section and displays the section name in a text box.

3. Type the section name.

4. Tap an empty part of the new section. OneNote closes the text box.

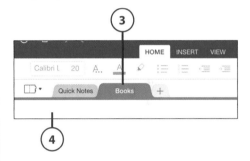

Rename a Section

If you made an error when you originally named a section, or if the section's current name no longer reflects the section's content, you can rename the section.

1. Double-tap the section tab. OneNote opens the tab text for editing.

2. To remove the existing name entirely, tap Cut. Otherwise, tap to the right of the first character you want to delete.

3. Edit the section name.

4. Tap an empty part of the new section. OneNote closes the text box.

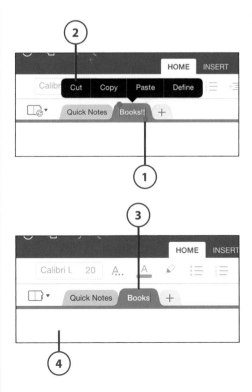

Working with Pages

After sections, the third level in the notebook organizational hierarchy is the page, which is more or less a blank slate into which you insert your OneNote data. Each section can have an unlimited number of pages, and the idea is that you use separate pages to break down each section into separate subtopics. Each page appears in the right pane of the notebook window.

Insert a New Page

Each new section you create comes with a new page, but you can add more pages whenever you need them.

1. Tap the tab of the section in which you want to insert the new page.

2. Tap Add Page. OneNote inserts a new page into the section.

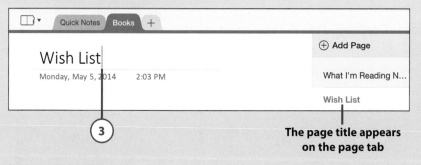

The page title appears on the page tab

3. Type the page title.

Change the Page Color

To give OneNote a splash of color, you can change the background of color of a page.

1. Tap the section that contains the page you want to format.

2. Tap the page tab.

3. Tap View.

4. Tap Page Color.

5. Tap the background color you want to apply.

Removing the Page Color

If you find that the page background color makes it harder to read your text, you can remove the color. Tap the page, tap View, tap Page Color, and then tap No Color.

Entering Text on a Page

Filling your pages with content is what OneNote is all about, and OneNote makes it easy to insert everything from simple typewritten notes, dates and times, image files, even screen captures. All OneNote content appears inside a container, which is essentially a box that surrounds the content.

Most page content consists of text notes, and OneNote makes it simple to add text to a page:

- For typewritten notes, tap where you want the note to appear and then start typing. OneNote immediately places a container around the text. When you're done, tap outside the container.

- To create a bulleted list, tap where you want the list to appear and then tap Home, Bullets. You can also tap Home, Numbering if you prefer a numbered list.

- To add text from another app, open the app, copy the text, return to OneNote, tap and hold for a few second inside the page where you want the text to appear, and then tap Paste to insert the copied text.

Insert the Date

Some of the content you add to a OneNote page will be date-sensitive. For such content, you should date-stamp the placeholder by inserting the current date.

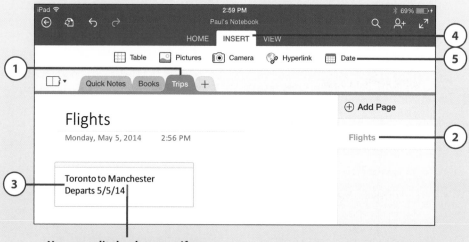

You can edit the date text if you
want to display a different date

1. Tap the section you want to use.

2. Tap the page you want to use.

3. Position the insertion point where you want to insert the date.

4. Tap the Insert tab.

5. Tap Date. OneNote inserts today's date.

Add a Link to a Website

OneNote comes with a Hyperlink command that enables you to insert links to websites. This is handy if you use your pages to store links to websites you visit often or want to visit in the future. (For the latter, apply the Web Site to Visit tag; see the section "Tag an Item," later in this chapter.)

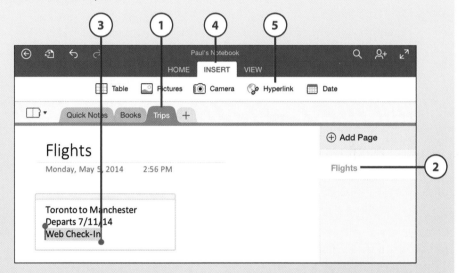

1. Tap the section you want to use.

2. Tap the page you want to use.

3. Select the text that you want to turn into a link. You can also position the insertion point where you want to insert new link text.

4. Tap the Insert tab.

5. Tap Hyperlink. OneNote displays the Insert Hyperlink dialog.

>>>Go Further
COPYING THE LINK ADDRESS

Although some web addresses are relatively short and therefore easily remembered and typed, most are not. In fact, it's common for modern web addresses to be both long and complex. This means that you can save yourself quite a bit of time and trouble by first copying the web address that you want to use for your link. Use Safari or another browser to navigate to the page, press and hold the address for a few seconds, and then tap Copy in the menu that appears when you release the screen.

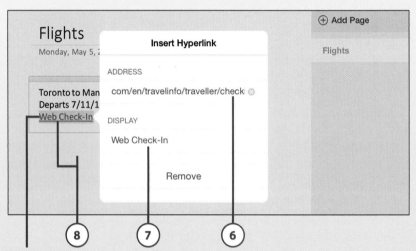

To open the link in Safari, tap the link and then tap Open

6. Type the link address.

7. If you didn't select text in advance, type the link text.

8. Tap outside the dialog. OneNote inserts the link.

Editing a Link
To make changes to a link, tap it to open the Hyperlink dialog, and then tap Edit.

Working with Page Containers

When you insert data on a page—whether it's text, a link, or an image—the data appears inside a special object called a container. When you have one or more containers on a page, working with the data is almost always straight-forward. For example, to edit container text, you select inside the container and change the existing text or add new text. To format the text, you select it and use the buttons on the Ribbon's Home tab.

If you use OneNote either on the desktop or in OneDrive, then you probably spend a significant amount of time adjusting containers to get the best or most efficient layout for your data. Unfortunately, OneNote for iPad offers only limited support for working with containers. For example, you can't move a container in OneNote for iPad, and the only way to change a container's size is to move the cursor to the end of the container and tap Return.

Sizing a Container
You can increase the size of a container by tapping just below it.

Building a OneNote Table

A typical notebook page, like a typical page in a paper notebook, is a jumble of text, with placeholders scattered around the page. This randomness isn't necessarily a bad thing because it's in keeping with OneNote's inherent infor-mality and (at least on the surface) structure-free format. However, there will be times when you want your notes to have some structure. If it's a list of items, you can insert a bulleted list into a placeholder (on the Home tab, tap Bullets); if it's an ordered sequence of items, use a numbered list instead (on the Home tab, tap Numbering).

However, you might have data that consists of multiple items, each of which has the same set of details. For example, you might want to record a list of upcoming flights, each of which has an airline name, flight number, depar-ture date and time, destination, arrival date and time, seat number, and so on.

For these kinds of data structures, you can insert a table into a container. A table is a rectangular structure with the following characteristics:

- Each item in the list gets its own horizontal rectangle called a *row*.

- Each set of details in the list gets its own vertical rectangle called a *column*.

- The rectangle formed by the intersection of a row and a column is called a *cell* and you use the table cells to hold the data.

In other words, a OneNote table is similar to a Word table, which is discussed in Chapter 5, "Working with Page Layout and Design in Word").

Insert a Table

To create a table in OneNote, you first insert a default table and then edit that table as required.

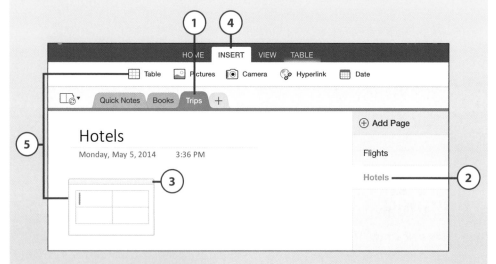

1. Tap the section you want to use.

2. Tap the page you want to use.

3. Tap where you want the table to appear.

4. Tap the Insert tab.

5. Tap Table. OneNote inserts a default table with two rows and two columns.

**Use the commands on the Table tab to
select, insert, and delete table items**

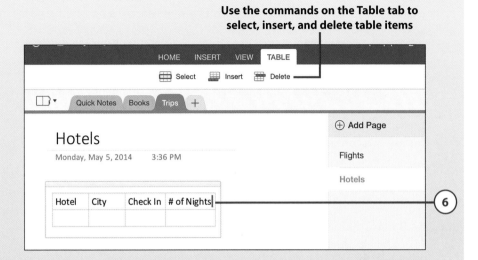

6. Tap inside a cell and then add the text that you want to store in the cell. Repeat for
   the other cells in the table.

Working with a OneNote Table

A OneNote table is similar to a Word table, so you can use the same techniques to add
and delete rows and columns, select table items, and so on. See Chapter 5 for details.

Working with Tags

OneNote enables you to augment items in a page with small icons called
tags. For example, many tags can help you prioritize page data, including the
Important, Critical, and Question tags. Similarly, many tags can help you organize your data, including the Project A and Project B tags.

However, probably the most common use of tags is to set up a to-do list. One
of the secrets of productivity in a fast-paced, information-overloaded world is
organizing the things that require your attention and your effort in a way that
minimizes stress and maximizes efficiency. If you have a long list of things to
do, the worst way to handle the list is to keep it in your head. If you do this,
you'll not only worry about forgetting something, but you'll always have each
task rumbling around in your brain, so you'll jump from one to the other
rather than concentrating on a single task at a time. Plastering sticky notes

all over your monitor isn't much better because all the tasks are still "in your face," and you won't be much better off.

The best way to organize a list of pending and current tasks is to have a single place where you record the tasks' particulars and can augment those particulars as things change and new data becomes available. This place must be one that you check regularly so that there's never a danger of overlooking a task, and ideally it should be a place where you can prioritize your tasks. This way, you can focus on a single task, knowing that everything you need to do is safely recorded and prioritized. As you've probably guessed by now, the place I'm talking about is OneNote, which is ideally suited to recording, organizing, and prioritizing tasks and to-do lists.

Tag an Item

You can apply a tag to a single item or to multiple items. You can also apply multiple tags to a single item.

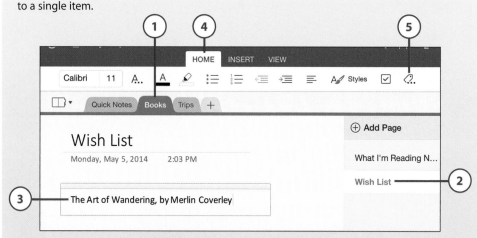

1. Tap the section that contains the page you want to work with.

2. Tap the page that contains the data you want to tag.

3. If you want to tag a specific paragraph within a text container, select inside that paragraph. If you want to apply the same tag to multiple paragraphs, select those paragraphs.

4. Tap the Home tab.

5. Tap Tag. OneNote displays the Tag gallery.

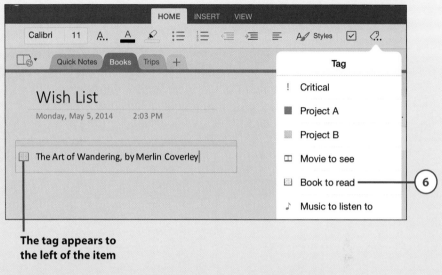

The tag appears to the left of the item

6. Tap the tag you want to use. OneNote applies the tag to the data.

Removing a Tag

To delete a tag you no longer need, position the insertion point at the beginning of the paragraph; then tap the Delete key.

Building Lists

To-do lists are an important part of OneNote, and part of the evidence for that is the large number of check box-like tags it offers. In addition to the standard To Do tag, there are six others:

- Discuss with Manager

- Schedule Meeting

- Call Back

- To Do Priority 1

- To Do Priority 2

- Client Request

Each of these tags gives you a check box augmented with a small icon. When you complete a task, you select the check box to place a red check mark inside, which gives you a strong visual clue about which tasks are done and which are still pending.

Create a To-Do List

You create a OneNote to-do list by building a list and then tagging it using the To Do tag.

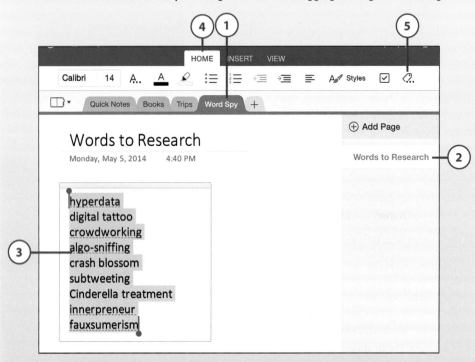

1. Tap the section that contains the page you want to work with.

2. Tap the page where you want your to-do list to appear.

3. Select all the items in your to-do list.

4. Tap the Home tab.

5. Tap Tag. OneNote displays the Tag gallery.

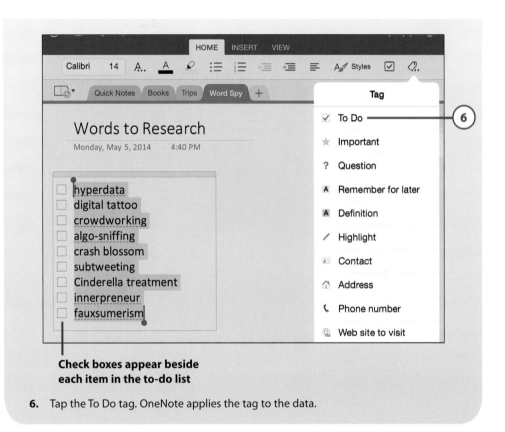

**Check boxes appear beside
each item in the to-do list**

6. Tap the To Do tag. OneNote applies the tag to the data.

Working with Notebooks

The hierarchical structure of a OneNote notebook means that you can break
down your data in a number of ways. That is, you can assign major topics
their own sections and then subdivide each topic into multiple pages within
a section. That works well for most people, and it's common to use only a single notebook. However, you might find that your notebook has so many sections that it has become difficult to navigate and to find the data you need.
In that case, you might consider creating a second notebook. For example,
many people maintain one notebook for personal data and another for business data. Similarly, if you share your iPad with other people, then you'll no
doubt prefer that everyone use their own notebook.

Create a New Notebook

You can create a new notebook either locally on your PC or remotely on your OneDrive.

1. Tap Back.

2. Tap Notebooks.

3. Tap Create Notebook.

4. Type a name for the notebook.

5. Tap Create. OneNote creates the new notebook and opens it.

Deleting a Notebook

If you no longer need a particular notebook, you can't delete it from OneNote for iPad. Instead, you need to use either the desktop version of OneNote or your OneDrive.

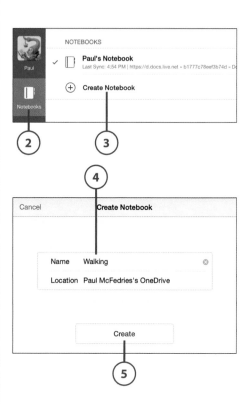

Switch Between Notebooks

When you have two or more notebooks open, OneNote gives you a quick and easy method for switching from one to another.

1. Tap Notebooks. OneNote displays the Notebooks pane.

2. Tap the notebook you want to use. OneNote switches to that workbook.

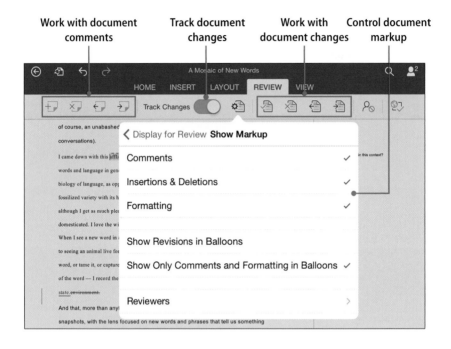

Work with document comments

Track document changes

Work with document changes

Control document markup

In this chapter, you learn how to collaborate with other people, particularly on Word and Excel files.

→ Inserting and working with comments in Word
→ Tracking changes to Word documents
→ Viewing Excel comments
→ Deleting Excel comments
→ Sharing a link to a document

12

Collaborating with Others

Whether you're a company employee, a consultant, or a freelancer, you almost certainly work with other people in one capacity or another. Most of the time, our work with others is informal and consists of ideas exchanged during meetings, phone calls, or email messages. However, we're often called upon to work with others more closely by collaborating with them on a document. This could involve commenting on another person's work, editing someone else's document, or dividing a project among multiple authors. For all these situations, Office for iPad offers a number of powerful collaborative tools. This chapter shows you how to use and get the most out of these tools.

Collaborating in Word with Comments and Changes

Word is the collaboration champion in the Office for iPad suite because, more than any other Office program, Word boasts an impressive collection of tools that enables you to work with other people on a document. In the next few sections, you learn about the simplest and most common collaboration tools: comments and tracking changes.

Insert Comments in a Word Document

If someone asks for your feedback on a document, you could write that feedback in a separate document or in an email message. However, feedback is most useful when it appears in the proper context. That is, if you have a suggestion or critique of a particular word, sentence, or paragraph, the reader will understand that feedback more readily if it appears near the text in question. To do that in Word, you insert a comment, a separate section of text that is associated with some part of the original document.

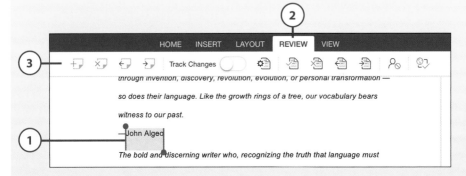

1. Select the text you want to comment on. If you want to comment on a particular word, you can position the cursor within or immediately to the left or right of the word.

2. Tap the Review tab.

3. Tap New Comment. Word highlights the selected text to indicate that it has an associated comment.

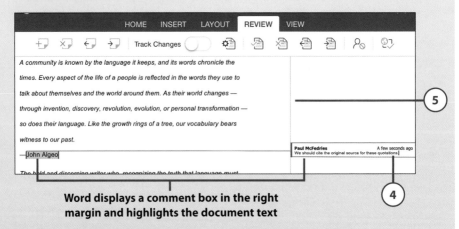

Word displays a comment box in the right margin and highlights the document text

4. Type the comment.

5. Tap outside the comment area.

Edit a Comment

You can edit a comment either by adding to or changing the existing comment text, or by responding to a comment made by another person.

1. Tap the comment you want to edit. The Comments box appears.

2. Edit the comment text as needed.

3. Tap outside the comment box.

Delete a Comment

When you no longer need a comment, you can delete it to reduce clutter in the Word document.

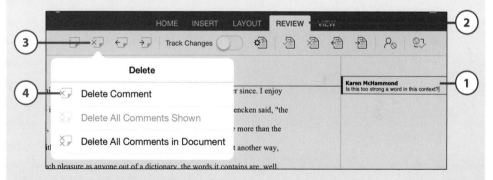

1. Tap the comment you want to delete.

2. Tap the Review tab.

3. Tap the Delete Comment button.

4. Tap Delete Comment.

Deleting All Comments

If you want a fresh start with a Word document, you can delete all the comments. Tap the Review tab, tap the Delete Comment button, and then tap Delete All Comments in Document.

Track Changes in a Word Document

A higher level of collaboration occurs when you ask another person to make changes to a document. That is, rather than suggesting changes by using comments, the other person performs the actual changes. How do you know what changes that person made? By using Word's Track Changes feature. When this feature is activated, Word keeps track of all changes to the original text—including adding, editing, deleting, and formatting the text. Track Changes shows not only what changes were made, but who made them and when.

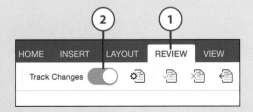

1. Tap the Review tab.
2. Tap the Track Changes switch to On.

Controlling the Display of Comments and Changes

Depending on the document and the number of reviewers, the comments and changes can make a document appear to be quite a mess. Fortunately, Word allows you to filter out particular types of changes, and even changes made by particular reviewers.

These filters are part of Word's Show Markup list, which contains the following six commands that toggle the respective markup on and off:

Defining Markup

Markup refers to the icons, font changes, and balloons that indicate the comments and changes reviewers have made to a document.

- **Comments**—Tap this command to toggle the display of comments.

- **Insertions and Deletions**—Tap this command to toggle the display of text added to and removed from the document.

- **Formatting**—Tap this command to toggle the display of format changes.

- **Show Revisions in Balloons**—Tap this command to display all the document revisions in the balloons that appears in the right margin.

- **Show Revisions in Balloons**—Tap this command to display only comments and formatting changes in the right margin.

- **Reviewers**—Tap this command to display a list of reviewers so that you can toggle the display of changes made by a particular reviewer.

Word also offers several options for controlling the entire markup in a document. The Display for Review list contains the following four commands:

- **All Markup**—This view shows the final version of the document (the version of the document if you accept all the current changes) with deletions marked as strikethrough, and comments, additions, and formatting changes shown in balloons in the right margin.

- **No Markup**—This view shows the final version of the document with none of the markup showing (that is, how the document would look if all the changes had been accepted).

- **Original with Markup**—This view shows the original version of the document with the markup displayed in the right margin.

- **Original**—This is the original version of the document, before any changes were made (or, more precisely, either before Track Changes was turned on or since the last time all the changes were accepted).

Control the Markup Display

By default, Word shows all revisions from all reviewers using the Simple Markup display, but you can change these defaults to ones that you prefer.

1. Tap the Review tab.

2. Tap Display for Review.

3. Tap how you want Word to display the document's markup.

4. Tap Show Markup.

5. Tap which types of markup you want to view.

6. Tap Reviewers.

7. Tap a reviewer to hide that person's markup.

Navigate Comments and Changes

To make sure that you review every comment or change in a document, or to accept or reject comments and changes individually (see the next section), you need to use Word's reviewing navigation tools.

1. Tap the Review tab.

2. Tap Next Comment to view the next comment in the document.

3. Tap Previous Comment to view the previous comment in the document.

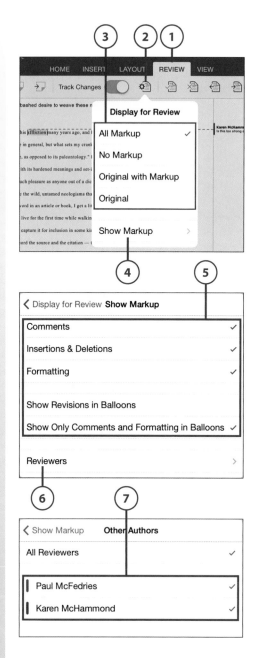

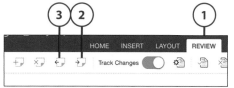

4. Tap Next Change to view the next revision in the document.

5. Tap Previous Change to view the previous revision in the document.

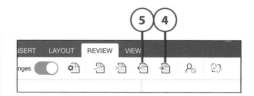

Accept or Reject Comments and Changes

The point of marking up a document is to review the changes and then either incorporate some or all of them into the final version or remove those that are not useful or suitable. Word gives you several tools to either accept the markup (this action applies to changes only) or reject the markup (this action applies to both comments and changes).

1. Tap the Review tab.

2. Navigate to the change you want to work with.

3. If you want to accept the change, tap the Accept button.

4. Tap Accept & Move to Next. If you don't want to automatically move to the next change, tap Accept Change.

5. If you want to reject the change, tap the Reject button.

6. Tap Reject & Move to Next. If you don't want to automatically move to the next change, tap Reject This Change.

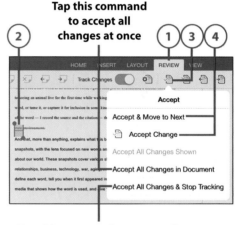

Tap this command to accept all changes at once

Tap this command to accept all changes and turn off Track Changes

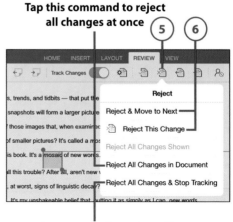

Tap this command to reject all changes at once

Tap this command to reject all changes and turn off Track Changes

>>>*Go Further*

ACCEPTING SHOWN CHANGES

In many situations, you want to accept all changes of a certain type (such as formatting or insertions and deletions) and review the rest. To accept all changes of a certain type, first use the Show Markup list to turn off the display of all revisions except the type you want to accept (see "Controlling the Display of Comments and Changes," earlier in this chapter). Then, in the Review tab, tap the Accept button and then tap Accept All Changes Shown. You can also accept only the changes made by a particular reviewer. To display the markup for a single reviewer, tap the Review tab, tap Display for Review, tap Show Markup, tap Reviewers, and then tap All Reviewers to turn off all markup. Tap the reviewer whose markup you want to accept. Tap Accept and then tap Accept All Changes Shown.

Collaborating in Excel with Comments

The simplest level of collaboration with an Excel workbook is the comment. This is a short snippet of text that you associate with a worksheet cell without it affecting the cell data. Instead, it's a separate text object that usually offers notes, suggestions, and critiques of the worksheet content.

View a Cell's Comment

By default, Excel indicates commented cells by placing a small, red triangle in the upper-right corner of the cell, but it doesn't display the comment itself. So to read a cell's comment, you must display it by hand.

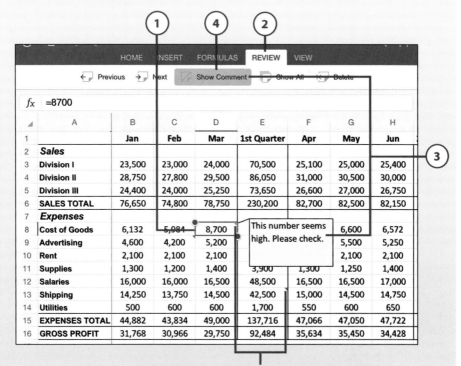

Excel indicates a comment by displaying a small
red triangle in the upper-right corner of the cell

1. Tap the cell that contains the comment you want to view.

2. Tap the Review tab.

3. Tap Show Comment. Excel displays the comment.

4. To hide the comment, tap the Show Comment command again to deactivate it.

Inserting a Comment

Excel for iPad does not support adding new comments. To annotate a workbook with comments, you must use either a desktop version of Excel or Excel Online.

Navigate Workbook Comments

If the worksheet has multiple comments, you can quickly navigate from one comment to another, which is usually faster than displaying individual comments.

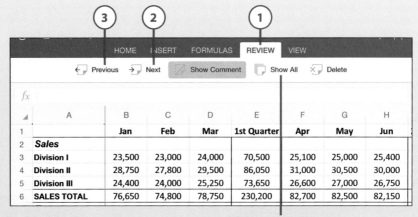

If there are multiple comments, you can display them all by tapping Show All

1. Tap the Review tab.

2. Tap Next to view the next comment in the worksheet.

3. Tap Previous to view the previous comment in the worksheet.

Delete a Workbook Comment

If your workbook contains a comment you no longer need, you should delete it to reduce the worksheet's visual clutter and to make it easier to navigate the other comments.

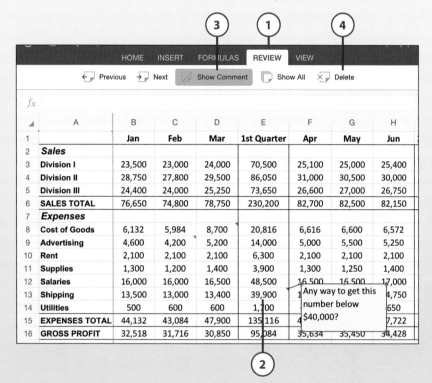

1. Tap the Review tab.

2. Tap the cell that contains the comment you want to delete.

3. Tap Show Comment to display the comment and confirm that it is the one you want to remove.

4. Tap Delete.

Sharing a Document

If you work with a document online via OneDrive, you can share that document with other people. Office for iPad gives you two ways to share a document:

- **Using email**—In this case you send an email message to one or more recipients, and that message contains a link to a OneDrive location of the document you're sharing.

- **Using a link**—In this case you copy a OneDrive address (Office for iPad calls it a link) for the document you want to share. You can then distribute that address to the people you want to collaborate with (via email, text message, online post, or whatever).

In both cases, you can set up the shared document for viewing only, or to allow editing.

Email a Link to a Shared Document

To allow other people to view, comment on, or even edit a document on your OneDrive, you can send an email that contains a link to the document's OneDrive location.

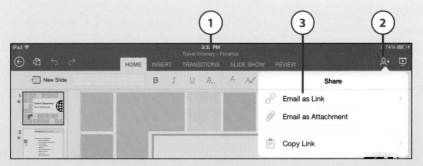

1. Open the document you want to share.
2. Tap Share.
3. Tap Email as Link.

Email as Link Is Disabled
You can only email a link to a document that's stored on your OneDrive. If the Email as Link command is disabled, it means you're working with a document that's stored locally on your iPad.

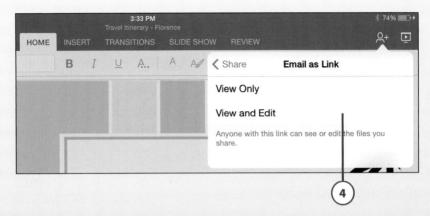

4. Tap how you want the document shared. The app generates a OneDrive address for the document and then displays an email message.

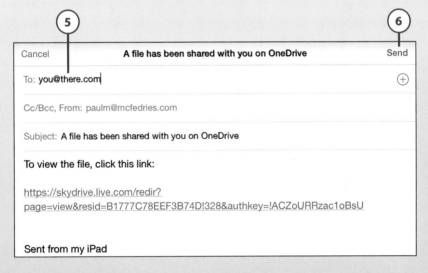

5. Choose your recipients.

6. Tap Send.

Copy a Link to a Shared Document

If you want more flexibility when it comes to sharing a document, you can copy a link to a OneDrive address for that document, which you can then distribute to your collaborators.

1. Open the document you want to share.

2. Tap Share.

3. Tap Copy Link.

Copy Link Is Disabled

You can only copy a link to a document that's stored online within a OneDrive folder. If you're working with a document that's stored on your iPad, the Copy Link command will be disabled.

4. Tap how you want the document shared. The app generates a OneDrive address for the document and then copies the address. You can then paste the address in whatever medium you want to use to share the link.

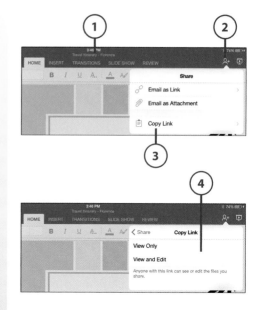

Create new   Navigate   Share   Configure
documents   folders   documents   your profile

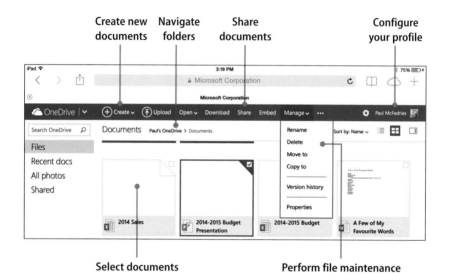

Select documents   Perform file maintenance

In this chapter, you learn everything you need to know about configuring and using OneDrive.

→ Changing your Windows Live display name and profile picture

→ Viewing, navigating, creating, and deleting OneDrive folders

→ Creating, viewing, and editing Office documents on OneDrive

→ Moving, copying, renaming, and deleting OneDrive files

→ Sharing and adding comments to documents on OneDrive

Learning OneDrive Essentials

If you'll be storing your Office for iPad documents online using OneDrive, then you'll get much more out of the Office for iPad apps if you familiarize yourself with all of OneDrive's features and options. That's just what you'll do in this chapter, as I take your through a complete tour of OneDrive, with an emphasis on using it with the Office for iPad apps. You'll learn some useful options for configuring and customizing OneDrive, and then you'll go through all the essential tasks for working with OneDrive folders and files, as well as uploading Office documents and viewing and editing those documents using the Office Online apps.

Setting Up OneDrive

Before getting to the bread-and-butter tasks, let's start by looking at a couple techniques for setting up OneDrive to suit your style. (More accurately, I should say that these are techniques for setting up Windows Live to suit your style because each applies to all the Windows Live pages, not just OneDrive.)

First, here's a quick reminder about how you access OneDrive on your iPad:

- Use Safari to navigate to https://onedrive.live.com and then log in.

- If you're already on another Windows Live site—such as People (https://people.live.com) or Outlook.com (https://mail.live.com)—tap More (the downward-pointing arrow in the upper-left corner of the browser screen) and then tap OneDrive.

Either way, you end up at the OneDrive Files page, which shows your folders, how much storage space you have left, and so on.

Change Your Display Name

The live.com sites offer only a few configuration options, one of which is to change your display name. This name appears in the upper-right corner of each live.com screen, and in the Account popover that appears when you tap your user account in any Office for iPad app.

1. Tap your current display name.

2. Tap Edit Profile. The Profile page appears.

3. Tap Edit beside your display name.

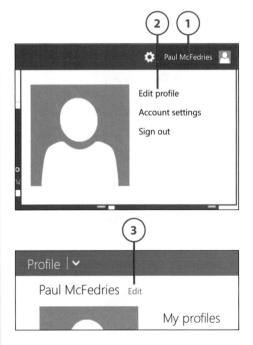

4. Edit the name you want to display.

5. Tap Save.

More Than OneDrive

Remember that your display name applies to *all* the services that are associated with your Microsoft account. Therefore, changing your display name here also affects the display name that appears in those other services.

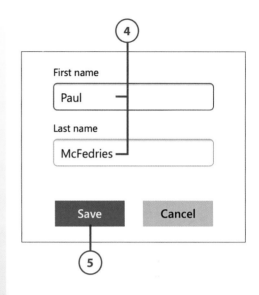

Assign a Picture to Your Profile

Your display name adds a personal touch, but what's not so personal is the generic "user" icon that appears along with your display name. You can change that default icon to something more pleasant and personal.

1. Tap your current display name.

2. Tap Edit Profile. The Profile page appears.

3. Tap Change Picture.

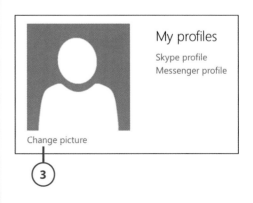

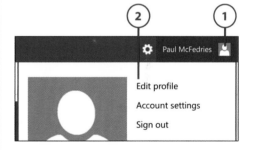

4. Tap Choose File.

5. Tap Choose Existing.

6. Tap the album that contains the picture you want to use.

7. Tap the picture you want to use.

More Than OneDrive

As with the display name, bear in mind that the picture you apply to your profile will appear in every service and product that's linked to your Microsoft account.

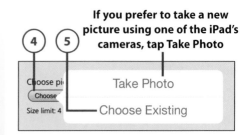

If you prefer to take a new picture using one of the iPad's cameras, tap Take Photo

8. Tap Save.

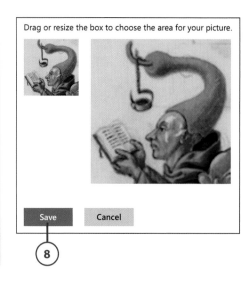

Drag or resize the box to choose the area for your picture.

Save   Cancel

⑧

>>>Go Further

GETTING A PICTURE ONTO YOUR IPAD

You normally add photos to your iPad by syncing images from your Mac or PC to your device. However, a sync is overkill if you just need a single image to use for your profile picture. A faster method is to attach the picture to an email and send the message to an account that's set up on your iPad. Open Mail, tap the message, tap and hold the picture for a few seconds, and then tap Save Image. This saves the picture to your iPad's Camera Roll album.

Working with OneDrive Folders

OneDrive is an online storage application that acts as a kind of cloud-based hard drive that you can use to store any type of file, including Office Web App files. The default size of your OneDrive is 7 GB, so you probably won't be able to upload all your stuff to OneDrive, but there's lots of room for files you want to store online. (You can also upgrade your storage to 50 GB for $25 per year; 100 GB for $50 per year; or 200 GB for $100 per year.)

Just as your computer's hard drive comes with different folders for storing different types of files, so too does your OneDrive come with folders for online file storage.

The default OneDrive comes with four folders:

- **Documents**—This is the standard folder for storing files. By default, only you can view the contents of this folder.

- **Music**—You use this folder to store music files. By default, only you can view the contents of this folder.

- **Pictures**—You use this folder to store picture files. By default, only you can view the contents of this folder.

- **Public**—You can use this folder to store any type of file, but the contents of the file are viewable by anyone with Internet access. (So be careful what you upload!)

In this section, you learn all about working with folders in OneDrive: viewing folders, navigating the folder hierarchy, creating your own folders, changing the folder view, and deleting folders.

View a OneDrive Folder

To work with a document on your OneDrive, you first must open the folder where the file is stored.

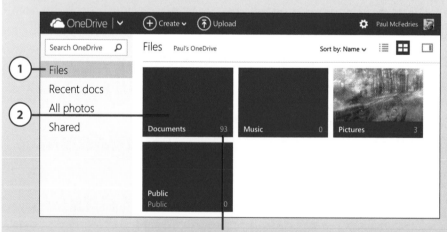

**This number tells you how many objects
(subfolders and files) are in the folder**

1. Tap Files.

2. Tap the folder you want to view. OneDrive displays the contents of that folder.

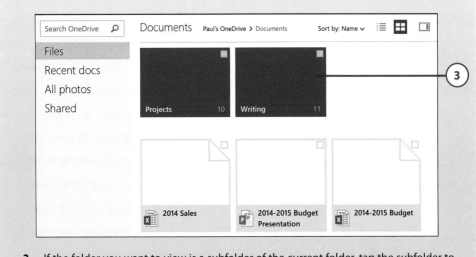

3. If the folder you want to view is a subfolder of the current folder, tap the subfolder to open it.

Navigate OneDrive Folders

Opening OneDrive folders is much like opening folders on a local computer because you drill down into the folders, subfolders, and so on. You can work back up the folder hierarchy by tapping the browser's Back button, but that's not efficient if you have to work back several levels. A better way is to take advantage of the "breadcrumb" path that appears at the top of the folder area.

1. Tap the name of the folder to which you want to navigate. OneDrive takes you directly to that folder.

Landscape Orientation

If you've drilled down several levels in your folder hierarchy, the breadcrumb path might get cut off when your iPad is in portrait orientation. To see the full breadcrumb path, rotate your iPad into landscape orientation.

>>>Go Further

BREADCRUMB PATH

A *breadcrumb path* is a navigation feature that displays a list of the places a person has visited or the route a person has taken. The term comes from the Brothers Grimm fairy tale Hansel and Gretel, who threw down bits of bread to help find their way out of the forest. This feature is common on websites where the content is organized as a hierarchy or as a sequence of pages. In OneDrive, the breadcrumb path shows you the hierarchical path you've taken to get to the current folder. The breadcrumb path lets you know exactly where you are in OneDrive, which is nice, but OneDrive also adds interactivity to the breadcrumb path by turning the folder names into links. You can navigate back to any part of the hierarchy by tapping the folder name in the breadcrumb path.

Create a OneDrive Folder

The default OneDrive folders might be all you need, but if not OneDrive lets you create your own folders. You can either add a main folder to the OneDrive home page (so you see the folder immediately when you log in to OneDrive and select the Files link; this is the way to go if you'll be accessing the folder often and want quick access to it), or you can add a subfolder to any existing folder.

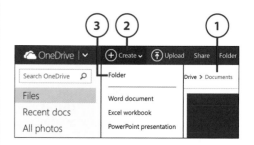

1. Navigate to the folder in which you want to create the new folder.

2. Tap Create.

3. Tap Folder. OneDrive displays the Create Folder dialog box.

4. Type the name of the new folder.

5. Tap Create. OneDrive creates the folder and then displays it.

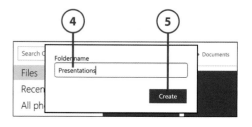

Change the OneDrive Folder View

OneDrive folders open in Thumbnail view, by default, which means that, for certain file types (particularly Office documents), you see a thumbnail version of the file contents. OneDrive also offers Details view, which shows the file contents as a four-column list: the file-name, the date and time the file was last modified, whether the file is shared, and the file size. Depending on what you want to see in a folder, you can switch between these views.

1. Open the OneDrive folder you want to work with.

2. Tap the view setting you want to use: Icons, Details, or Thumbnails.

You can also tap Details Pane to see extra details about the selected file

Thumbnails View

Details View

Use this list to sort the folder contents

Delete a OneDrive Folder

If you have a OneDrive folder that you no longer use, it's a good idea to delete it to reduce the clutter on either your OneDrive home page or in the folder where the unused folder resides. You may also need to delete one or more folders if you find that you're running out of room in your OneDrive.

1. Navigate to the folder want to delete.

2. Tap Folder Actions.

3. Tap Delete Folder. OneDrive deletes the folder and any files it contains and drops you off at the parent folder.

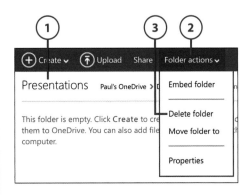

It's Not All Good

Double-Check Before Deleting

At this point, it's a good idea to double-check that the folder doesn't contain any files you want to keep because OneDrive doesn't ask you to confirm the deletion. If the folder contains a file you want to preserve, you should move the file to another folder (see "Move a OneDrive File to Another Folder" later in this chapter).

Undoing a Deletion

If you delete a folder and then immediately realize your mistake, tap the Undo command that appears for a few seconds after the deletion is complete. If that command no longer appears, tap the Recycle Bin link that appears in the lower-left corner of the window, select the folder's check box, and then tap Restore.

Working with Office Documents in OneDrive

Now that you have your OneDrive home configured and your folders set up, it's time to start working with documents in OneDrive. I'll show you a few key techniques for dealing with Office documents online, including creating new Office documents in OneDrive, opening OneDrive documents using the online Office apps and sending OneDrive documents to the Office for iPad apps.

Create a New Office Document in OneDrive

Although you'll likely create your Office documents in the convenient confines of your iPad, if you happen to be logged in to Windows Live, you can craft a new document directly in a OneDrive folder. You can create a Word document, an Excel workbook, a PowerPoint presentation, or a OneNote notebook.

1. Navigate to the folder where you want to store the new document.

2. Tap Create. OneDrive displays a list of Office file types.

3. Tap the type of Office document you want to create. OneDrive creates the new document and opens it in the associated Office app, which appears in a new browser tab.

4. Tap the document name (which is a generic name such as Document1) and then type a name for the document.

5. Tap outside the name box (or tap Return on the keyboard) to set the document name.

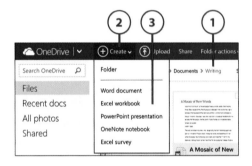

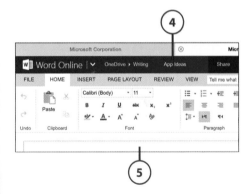

Viewing Documents Online

After you've populated your OneDrive folders with Office documents, you're ready to start working with those documents online. The easiest way to work with an Office document is simply to view the document's contents, without editing the data. In view mode, you can perform the following actions in the Office Online apps:

- **Word Online**—You can scroll through the document one page at a time, and you can zoom in or out of the document.

- **Excel Online**—You can scroll through the current worksheet and navigate from one worksheet to another by tapping the worksheet tabs. In a worksheet, you can adjust the row heights and column widths. You can also refresh the workbook's data connections and calculations.

- **PowerPoint Online**—You can scroll through a presentation's slides and view the notes associated with each slide. You can also run the presentation's slide show.

- **OneNote Online**—You can scroll through the current page, view a different page, and navigate from one notebook section to another by tapping the section tabs.

- **All Office Online apps**—You can tap Find to locate text within the document; you can tap Comments to see the comments that have been added to the document; you can tap Share to share the document with other people; and you can tap File to perform file-related tasks.

View a OneDrive Document

If you don't need to make changes to a document, you can open a read-only copy online using the associated Office Online app.

1. Navigate to the folder that contains the document.

2. Tap the document. OneDrive opens the document in a new tab.

3. When you are done viewing the document, close the tab.

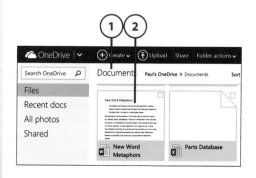

Automatic Edit Mode

Some Office file types don't support view mode, so when you tap such a document, OneDrive automatically opens the file in edit mode.

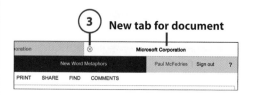

New tab for document

Edit a OneDrive Document Online

You can open and edit a OneDrive document within the web browser by loading the document into the associated Office Online app and then switching the document to edit mode.

1. Navigate to the folder that contains the document.

2. Tap the document. OneDrive opens a read-only copy of the document in a new tab.

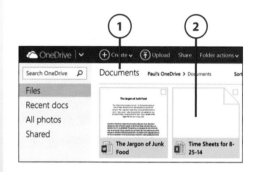

Unsupported Features

If the document you open contains features that are incompatible with the associated Office Online app, you might see a dialog box letting you know. In that case, you can either tap Cancel to open the document read-only, or tap Edit in the Browser to open the document for editing.

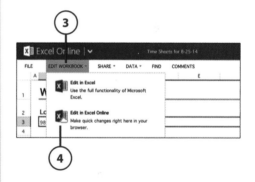

3. Tap Edit *File Type*, where *File Type* is the document type (such as Document or Workbook).

4. Tap Edit in *App* Online, where *App* is the name of the Office Online app (such as Word or Excel).

Edit a OneDrive Document on Your iPad

If you'd rather edit a OneDrive document using the associated Office for iPad app, you can open the document for viewing and then send the document to the iPad app.

1. Navigate to the folder that contains the document.

2. Tap the document. OneDrive opens a read-only copy of the document in a new tab.

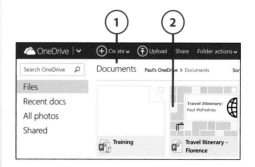

Unsupported Features

If the document you open contains features that are incompatible with the associated Office Online app, you might see a dialog box letting you know. In that case, be sure to tap Cancel to open the document in view mode.

3. Tap Edit *File Type*, where *File Type* is the document type (such as Document or Presentation).

4. Tap Edit in *App*, where *App* is the name of the Office for iPad app (such as Word or PowerPoint).

Working with OneDrive Files

If you've created some Office documents in OneDrive and uploaded a document or three to your OneDrive folders, now would be an excellent time to learn the basics of handling files in OneDrive. In the next few sections, you'll learn handy OneDrive techniques such as moving, copying, and renaming files; adding comments to a file; and deleting files from OneDrive.

Move a OneDrive File to Another Folder

After you create a file in, or save a file to, a OneDrive folder, you might later decide that the file resides in the wrong folder. In that case, OneDrive enables you to move the file to the folder you prefer.

1. Navigate to the OneDrive folder that contains the file you want to move.

2. Tap the file's check box to select the file.

Locating the Check Box

If the folder is currently in Thumbnail view, the document's check box appears in the upper-right corner of the file thumbnail; If the folder is currently in Details view, the check box appears to the left of the file icon.

---

3. Tap Manage.

4. Tap Move To. OneDrive prompts you to select the destination folder.

5. Tap the folder you want to use as the destination.

6. Tap Move. OneDrive moves the file from its current folder to the folder you selected.

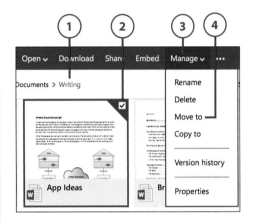

You can also tap New Folder if you want to create a folder

Copy a OneDrive File to Another Folder

Although you generally don't want the confusion of having multiple copies of a file floating around your OneDrive folders, there are a few scenarios where this is handy. For example, if you require a new file that is similar to an existing file, you can make a copy of the existing file and then edit the copy so that you don't have to re-create the file from scratch. Similarly, if you want to allow other people to open a file for editing but you also want to preserve the current version of the file, you could copy the file to another file that people have permission to edit.

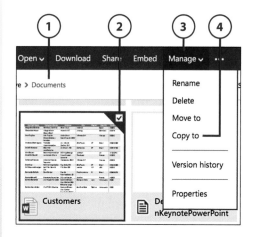

1. Navigate to the OneDrive folder that contains the file you want to copy.

2. Tap the file's check box to select the file.

3. Tap Manage.

4. Tap Copy To. OneDrive prompts you to select the destination folder.

5. Tap the folder you want to use as the destination.

6. Tap Copy. OneDrive places a copy of the file in the folder you selected.

You can also tap New Folder if you want to create a folder

Rename a OneDrive File

You probably rename files regularly on your computer's hard drive, so you know that it's a handy technique if the current name of a file is incorrect or doesn't reflect the file's contents. Fortunately, that same usefulness extends into the cloud because you can rename any file in a OneDrive folder.

1. Open the OneDrive folder that contains the document you want to rename.

2. Tap the file's check box to select the file.

3. Tap Manage.

4. Tap Rename. OneDrive opens the filename for editing.

5. Tap inside the filename box.

6. Edit the name.

7. Tap outside the filename box (or tap Return on the keyboard) to set the new name.

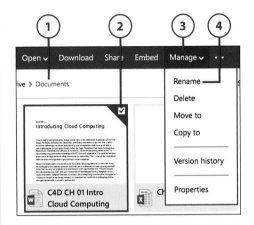

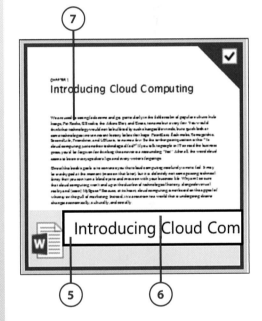

Delete a OneDrive File

If you no longer need a particular OneDrive file, you should delete it to reduce the clutter in the file's OneDrive folder. You also might want to delete a file if you're running low on OneDrive storage space.

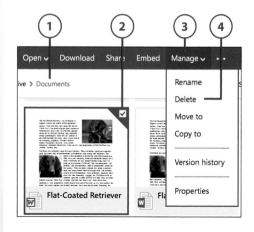

1. Open the OneDrive folder that contains the file you want to delete.

2. Tap the file's check box to select it.

3. Tap Manage.

4. Tap Delete. OneDrive removes the file.

Undoing the Deletion

If you delete a file by accident, tap the Undo command that appears for a few seconds after the deletion is complete. If that command no longer appears, tap the Recycle Bin link that appears in the lower-left corner of the window, select the file's check box, and then tap Restore.

It's Not All Good

Double-Check Before Deleting

Before proceeding with the deletion, it's a good idea to double-check that the file isn't one you want to keep because OneDrive doesn't ask you to confirm the deletion.

Collaborating with OneDrive

To collaborate on a document with other people, one prerequisite (and an obvious one, at that) is that you all have access to the document. That's tough to do on an iPad, but OneDrive is on the web, so in theory it can be accessed by anyone online. In practice, however, you need to explicitly share your document with others to give them access. OneDrive gives you two ways to share a document or folder:

- **Send an invitation**—In this case you send an email message to one or more recipients, and that message contains a link to the document or folder you're sharing.

- **Create a link**—In this case you use OneDrive to generate an address (OneDrive calls it a link) for the document or folder you want to share. You can then distribute that address to the people you want to collaborate with (via email, text message, online post, or whatever).

In both cases, you can set up the shared document or folder for viewing only, or to allow editing.

After you've shared a document, others can then open it and, whether the file is shared as read-only or for editing, add comments.

Send an Invitation to Share a OneDrive Document or Folder

To allow other people to view, comment on, or even edit a document on your OneDrive, you can send an invitation to share the document itself, or to share the folder that contains the document. Note that the latter technique enables people to access any document within the folder.

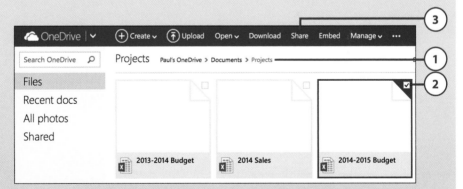

1. Open the OneDrive folder that you want to share or that contains the document you want to share.

2. If you're sharing one or more documents, tap to select the check box for each file.

3. Tap Share.

4. Tap inside the To box, begin typing the name of a recipient, and then tap the recipient when OneDrive recognizes the person from your list of contacts. Repeat as needed for each other person you want to invite.

Sharing with a Noncontact

To share the document or folder with someone not in your Contacts list, type that person's email address and press Return.

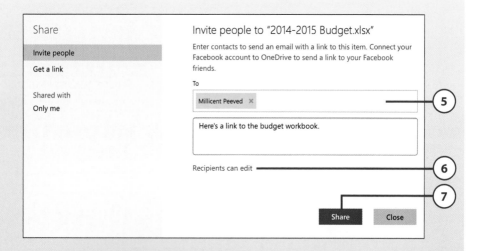

5. Type a brief note explaining the invitation.

6. If you want to allow the invitees to edit documents, tap Recipients Can Edit.

7. Tap Share. OneDrive sends the invitation to the recipients.

8. Tap Close.

>>>*Go Further*
REQUIRING A MICROSOFT ACCOUNT

For an extra level of security, you can specify that your recipients must log in using a Microsoft account. To set this up, tap Recipients Can Edit in the Share pane. In the two lists that appear, tap the lower list and then tap Recipients Need to Sign in with a Microsoft Account. If you don't want your recipients to edit your shared documents, tap the upper list and then tap Recipients Can Only View.

Create a Link to Share a OneDrive Document or Folder

If you want more flexibility for sharing a document or folder, you can use OneDrive to generate an address for that resource, which you can then distribute to your collaborators. Note that the Public folder is already set up with links to share (one that allows only viewing and one that allows editing), so it's often easiest to use that folder to share your documents.

1. Open the OneDrive folder that you want to share or that contains the document you want to share.

2. If you're sharing one or more documents, tap to select the check box for each file.

3. Tap Share.

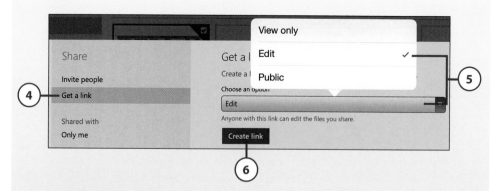

4. Tap Get a Link.

5. Tap the Choose an Option list, and then tap the type of access you want the link to provide.

6. Tap Create Link. OneDrive creates the link.

Copy this address and distribute it to your collaborators

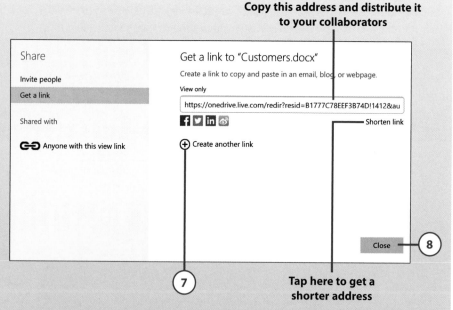

Tap here to get a shorter address

7. If you want to create another link for the same resources, tap Create Another Link, and then repeat steps 5 and 6.

8. Tap Close.

>>>Go Further
SHORTENING THE ADDRESS

OneDrive's shared addresses can be quite long—often more than 100 characters! That can be problematic in a tweet, text message, or other medium where space is at a premium. To cut the address down to size, tap the Shorten Link command that appears just below the address. This creates a new address of just over 20 characters, which is much easier for sharing.

Add a Comment When Viewing a Document

If you're accessing a OneDrive document as a read-only file in view mode, you can still add one or more comments to the document.

1. Open the folder that contains the document.

2. Tap the document. OneDrive opens the document in view mode.

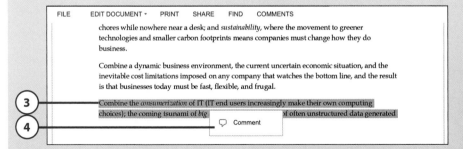

3. Select the document data on which you want to comment. OneDrive displays the Comment command.

4. Tap Comment. OneDrive displays the Comments pane and creates a blank comment.

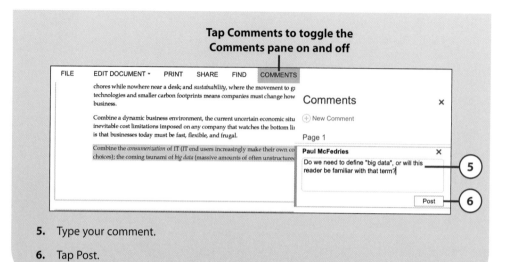

**Tap Comments to toggle the
Comments pane on and off**

5. Type your comment.

6. Tap Post.

>>>Go Further
REPLYING TO A COMMENT

If the document already has existing comments, you can reply to a comment.
This is useful if you want to answer a question or discuss a suggestion. Tap
Comments to open the Comments pane, tap the comment you want to work
with, and then tap the Reply icon. (Of the three comment icons that appear, it's
the one on the left.) Type your reply and then tap Post.

Add a Comment When Editing a Document

If you access a OneDrive document in editing mode, you can add one or more comments to the document.

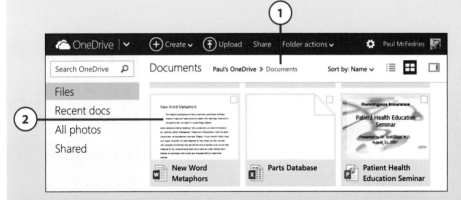

1. Navigate to the folder that contains the document.

2. Tap the document. OneDrive opens the document in view mode.

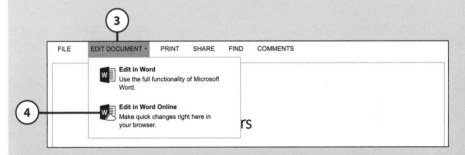

3. Tap Edit *File Type*, where *File Type* is the document type (such as Document).

4. Tap Edit in *App* Online, where *App* is the name of the Office Online app (such as Word).

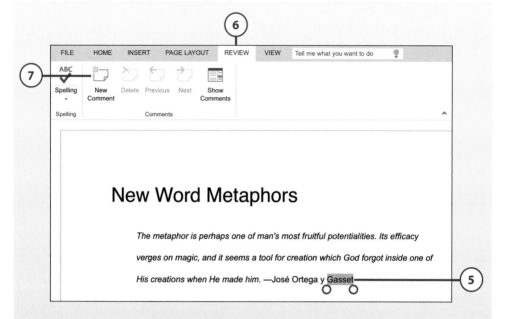

5. Select the document data on which you want to comment.

6. Tap the Review tab.

7. Tap New Comment. OneDrive displays the Comments pane and creates a blank comment.

Tap Show Comments to toggle the Comments pane on and off

8. Type your comment.

9. Tap Post.

A

Excel Worksheet Function Reference

As you learned in Chapter 6, "Entering Excel Data," to get to the real meat of a spreadsheet model, you need to expand your formula repertoire to include Excel's worksheet functions. Several hundred of these functions exist, and they're an essential part of making your worksheet work easier and more powerful. Excel has various function categories, including the following:

- Financial

- Logical

- Text

- Date and time

- Lookup and reference

- Math and trigonometry

- Statistical

- Engineering

- Info

- Database and list

(Note that this list, as well as the sections that follow, are presented in the order that the function category buttons appear in Excel for iPad's Formulas tab.)

Functions are formulas that Excel has predefined. They're designed to take you beyond the basic arithmetic and text formulas you've seen so far. They do this in three ways:

- Functions make simple but cumbersome formulas easier to use. For example, suppose that you want to add a list of 100 numbers in a column starting at cell A1 and finishing at cell A100. Even if you wanted to, you couldn't enter 100 separate additions in a cell because you would run out of room. (Recall that cells are limited to 255 characters.) Luckily, there's an alternative: the SUM() function. With this function, you can simply enter =SUM(A1:A100).

- Functions enable you to include complex mathematical expressions in your worksheets that otherwise would be difficult or impossible to construct using simple arithmetic operators. For example, determining a mortgage payment given the principal, interest, and term is a complicated matter, at best, but you can do it with Excel's PMT() function just by entering a few parameters.

- Functions enable you to include data in your applications that you couldn't access otherwise. For example, the INFO() function can tell you how much memory is available on your system, what operating system you're using, what version number it is, and more. Similarly, the powerful IF() function enables you to test the contents of a cell—for example, to see whether it contains a particular value or an error—and then perform an action accordingly, depending on the result.

As you can see, functions are a powerful addition to your worksheet-building arsenal. With proper use of these tools, there is no practical limit to the kinds of models you can create.

Every function has the same basic form:

```
FUNCTION(argument1, argument2, ...)
```

The *FUNCTION* part is just the name of the function, which always appears in uppercase letters (such as SUM or PMT). Note, however, that you don't need to type in the function name using uppercase letters. Whatever case you use, Excel automatically converts the name to all uppercase. In fact, it's good practice to enter function names using only lowercase letters. That way, if Excel doesn't convert the function name to uppercase, you know that it doesn't recognize the name, which means you probably misspelled it.

The items that appear within the parentheses and separated by commas are the function *arguments*. The arguments are the function's inputs—the data it uses to perform its calculations. With respect to arguments, functions come in two flavors:

- **No arguments**—Many functions don't require any arguments. For example, the NOW() function returns the current date and time, and doesn't require arguments.

- **One or more arguments**—Most functions accept at least 1 argument, and some accept as many as 9 or 10 arguments. These arguments fall into two categories: required and optional. The required arguments must appear between the parentheses, or the formula will generate an error. You use the optional arguments only if your formula needs them.

Let's look at an example. The FV() function determines the future value of a regular investment based on three required arguments and two optional ones:

```
FV(rate, nper, pmt, pv, type)
```

`rate`	The fixed rate of interest over the term of the investment.
`nper`	The number of deposits over the term of the investment.
`pmt`	The amount deposited each period.
`pv`	The present value of the investment. The default value is 0.
`type`	When the deposits are due (0 for the beginning of the period; 1 for the end of the period, which is the default).

This is called the function *syntax*. Three conventions are at work here and in Excel for iPad:

- *Italic type* indicates a placeholder. That is, when you use the function, you replace the placeholder with an actual value.

- Arguments shown in bold type are required.

- Arguments shown in regular type are optional.

For each required argument placeholder (and whatever optional argument you want to include), you substitute an appropriate value. For example, in the FV() function, you substitute *rate* with a decimal value between 0 and 1, *nper* with an integer, and *pmt* with a dollar amount. Arguments can take any of the following forms:

- Literal alphanumeric values

- Expressions

- Cell or range references

- Range names

- Arrays

- The result of another function

The function operates by processing the inputs and then returning a result. For example, the FV() function returns the total value of the investment at the end of the term.

Financial Functions

Excel is loaded with financial features that give you powerful tools for building models that manage both business and personal finances. You can use these functions to calculate such things as the monthly payment on a loan, the future value of an annuity, the internal rate of return of an investment, or the yearly depreciation of an asset.

Most of the formulas you'll work with will involve three factors—the *present value* (the amount something is worth now), the *future value* (the amount something is worth in the future), and the interest rate (or the discount rate)—plus two related factors: the *periods*, the number of payments or deposits over the term of the loan or investment, and the *payment*, the amount of money paid out or invested in each period.

When building your financial formulas, you need to ask yourself the following questions:

- Who or what is the subject of the formula? On a mortgage analysis, for example, are you performing the analysis on behalf of yourself or the bank?

- Which way is the money flowing with respect to the subject? For the present value, future value, and payment, enter money that the subject receives as a positive quantity, and enter money that the subject pays out as a negative quantity. For example, if you're the subject of a mortgage analysis, the loan principal (the present value) is a positive number because it's money that you receive from the bank; the payment and the remaining principal (the future value) are negative because they're amounts that you pay to the bank.

- What is the time unit? The underlying unit of both the interest rate and the period must be the same. For example, if you're working with the annual interest rate, you must express the period in years. Similarly, if you're working with monthly periods, you must use a monthly interest rate.

- When are the payments made? Excel differentiates between payments made at the end of each period and those made at the beginning.

Table A.1 gives you a list of all Excel's worksheet functions in the Financial category.

Table A.1. Excel's Financial Functions

Function	What It Does
ACCRINT	Calculates the accrued interest for a security that pays periodic interest
ACCRINTM	Calculates the accrued interest for a security that pays interest at maturity
AMORDEGRC	Calculates the depreciation for each accounting period by using a depreciation coefficient
AMORLINC	Calculates the depreciation for each accounting period
COUPDAYBS	Calculates the number of days from the beginning of the coupon period to the settlement date
COUPDAYS	Calculates the number of days in the coupon period that contains the settlement date
COUPDAYSNC	Calculates the number of days from the settlement date to the next coupon date

Function	What It Does
COUPNCD	Calculates the next coupon date after the settlement date
COUPNUM	Calculates the number of coupons payable between the settlement date and maturity date
COUPPCD	Calculates the previous coupon date before the settlement date
CUMIPMT	Calculates the cumulative interest paid between two periods
CUMPRINC	Calculates the cumulative principal paid on a loan between two periods
DB	Calculates the depreciation of an asset for a specified period by using the fixed-declining balance method
DDB	Calculates the depreciation of an asset for a specified period by using the double-declining balance method or some other method that you specify
DISC	Calculates the discount rate for a security
DOLLARDE	Converts a dollar price from a fractional value to a decimal value
DOLLARFR	Converts a dollar price from a decimal value to a fractional value
DURATION	Calculates the annual duration of a security with periodic interest payments
EFFECT	Calculates the effective annual interest rate
FV	Calculates the future value of an investment
FVSCHEDULE	Calculates the future value of an initial principal after applying a series of compound interest rates
INTRATE	Calculates the interest rate for a fully invested security
IPMT	Calculates the interest portion of a loan payment for a given loan period
IRR	Calculates the internal rate of return for a series of cash flows
ISPMT	Calculates the interest paid during a specific period of an investment
MDURATION	Calculates the Macauley modified duration for a security with an assumed par value of $100
MIRR	Calculates the internal rate of return where positive and negative cash flows are financed at different rates
NOMINAL	Calculates the annual nominal interest rate
NPER	Calculates the number of periods for a loan or investment
NPV	Calculates the net present value of an investment based on a series of periodic cash flows and a discount rate
ODDFPRICE	Calculates the price per $100 face value of a security with an odd first period
ODDFYIELD	Calculates the yield of a security with an odd first period

Function	What It Does
ODDLPRICE	Calculates the price per $100 face value of a security with an odd last period
ODDLYIELD	Calculates the yield of a security with an odd last period
PDURATION	Calculates the number of periods required by an investment to reach a specified value
PMT	Calculates the periodic payment for a loan or annuity
PPMT	Calculates the principle portion of a loan payment for a given loan period
PRICE	Calculates the price per $100 face value of a security that pays periodic interest
PRICEDISC	Calculates the price per $100 face value of a discounted security
PRICEMAT	Calculates the price per $100 face value of a security that pays interest at maturity
PV	Calculates the present value of an investment
RATE	Calculates the interest rate per period of a loan or annuity
RECEIVED	Calculates the amount received at maturity for a fully invested security
RRI	Calculates an equivalent interest rate for the growth of an investment
SLN	Calculates the straight-line depreciation of an asset for one period
SYD	Calculates the sum-of-years' digits depreciation of an asset for a specified period
TBILLEQ	Calculates the bond-equivalent yield for a Treasury bill
TBILLPRICE	Calculates the price per $100 face value for a Treasury bill
TBILLYIELD	Calculates the yield for a Treasury bill
VDB	Calculates the depreciation of an asset for a specified or partial period by using a declining balance method
XIRR	Calculates the internal rate of return for a schedule of cash flows that is not necessarily periodic
XNPV	Calculates the net present value for a schedule of cash flows that is not necessarily periodic
YIELD	Calculates the yield on a security that pays periodic interest
YIELDDISC	Calculates the annual yield for a discounted security; for example, a Treasury bill
YIELDMAT	Calculates the annual yield of a security that pays interest at maturity

Logical Functions

You can bring some measure of "intelligence" to your worksheets, meaning your formulas can test the values in cells and ranges, and then return results based on those tests. This is all done with Excel's logical functions, which are designed to create decision-making formulas. For example, you can test cell contents to see whether they're numbers or labels, or you can test formula results for errors. Table A.2 summarizes Excel's logical functions.

Table A.2. Excel's Logical Functions

Function	What It Does
AND	Returns TRUE if all the arguments are true
FALSE	Returns FALSE
IF	Performs a logical test and returns a value based on the result
IFERROR	Calculates a value you specify if a formula evaluates to an error; otherwise, returns the result of the formula
IFNA	Calculates the value you specify if a formula evaluates to #N/A; otherwise returns the result of the formula
NOT	Reverses the logical value of the argument
OR	Returns TRUE if any argument is true
TRUE	Returns TRUE
XOR	Calculates a logical exclusive OR of all arguments

Text Functions

In Excel, *text* is any collection of alphanumeric characters that isn't a numeric value, a date or time value, or a formula. Words, names, and labels are all obviously text values, but so are cell values preceded by an apostrophe (') or formatted as Text. Text values are also called *strings*. Text formulas consist only of the concatenation operator (&) used to combine two or more strings into a larger string.

Excel's text functions enable you to take text formulas to a more useful level by giving you numerous ways to manipulate strings. With these functions, you can convert numbers to strings, change lowercase letters to uppercase (and vice versa), compare two strings, and more. Table A.3 gives you a list of all Excel's worksheet functions in the Text category.

Table A.3. Excel's Text Functions

Function	What It Does
BAHTTEXT	Converts a number to text, using the baht currency format
CHAR	Calculates the character specified by the code number
CLEAN	Removes all nonprintable characters from a text string
CODE	Calculates a numeric code for the first character in a text string
CONCATENATE	Joins several text items into one text item
DBCS	Changes half-width (single-byte) English letters or katakana within a character string to full-width (double-byte) characters
DOLLAR	Converts a number to text, using the $ (dollar) currency format
EXACT	Checks to see if two text values are identical
FIND	Finds one text value within another (case-sensitive)
FIXED	Formats a number as text with a fixed number of decimals
LEFT	Calculates the leftmost characters from a text value
LEN	Calculates the number of characters in a text string
LOWER	Converts text to lowercase
MID	Calculates a specific number of characters from a text string starting at the position you specify
NUMBERVALUE	Converts text to number in a locale-independent manner
PROPER	Capitalizes the first letter in each word of a text value
REPLACE	Replaces characters within text
REPT	Repeats text a given number of times
RIGHT	Calculates the rightmost characters from a text value
SEARCH	Finds one text value within another (not case-sensitive)
SUBSTITUTE	Substitutes new text for old text in a text string
T	Converts its arguments to text
TEXT	Formats a number and converts it to text
TRIM	Removes spaces from text
UNICHAR	Calculates the Unicode character that is references by the given numeric value
UNICODE	Calculates the number (code point) that corresponds to the first character of the text
UPPER	Converts text to uppercase
VALUE	Converts a text argument to a number

Date and Time Functions

The date and time functions enable you to convert dates and times to serial numbers and perform operations on those numbers. This capability is useful for such things as accounts receivable aging, project scheduling, time-management applications, and much more.

Table A.4 gives you a list of all Excel's worksheet functions in the Date and Time category.

Table A.4. Excel's Date and Time Functions

Function	What It Does
DATE	Calculates the serial number of a particular date
DATEVALUE	Converts a date in the form of text to a serial number
DAY	Converts a serial number to a day of the month
DAYS	Calculates the number of days between two dates
DAYS360	Calculates the number of days between two dates based on a 360-day year
EDATE	Calculates the serial number of the date that is the indicated number of months before or after the start date
EOMONTH	Calculates the serial number of the last day of the month before or after a specified number of months
HOUR	Converts a serial number to an hour
ISOWEEKNUM	Calculates the number of the ISO week number of the year for a given date
MINUTE	Converts a serial number to a minute
MONTH	Converts a serial number to a month
NETWORKDAYS	Calculates the number of whole workdays between two dates
NETWORKDAYS.INTL	Calculates the number of whole workdays between two dates using parameters to indicate which and how many days are weekend days
NOW	Calculates the serial number of the current date and time
SECOND	Converts a serial number to a second
TIME	Calculates the serial number of a particular time
TIMEVALUE	Converts a time in the form of text to a serial number
TODAY	Calculates the serial number of today's date

Function	What It Does
WEEKDAY	Converts a serial number to a day of the week
WEEKNUM	Converts a serial number to a number representing where the week falls numerically with a year
WORKDAY	Calculates the serial number of the date before or after a specified number of workdays
WORKDAY.INTL	Calculates the serial number of the date before or after a specified number of workdays using parameters to indicate which and how many days are weekend days
YEAR	Converts a serial number to a year
YEARFRAC	Calculates the year fraction representing the number of whole days between start_date and end_date

Lookup and Reference Functions

Getting the meaning of a word in the dictionary is always a two-step process: First, you look up the word, and then you read its definition. This idea of looking something up to retrieve some related information is at the heart of many spreadsheet operations. For example, the value of one argument often depends on the value of another. Here are some examples:

- In a formula that calculates an invoice total, the customer's discount might depend on the number of units purchased.

- In a formula that charges interest on overdue accounts, the interest percentage might depend on the number of days each invoice is overdue.

- In a formula that calculates employee bonuses as a percentage of salary, the percentage might depend on how much the employee improved upon the given budget.

The usual way to handle these kinds of problems is to look up the appropriate value, and Excel offers a number of functions that enable you to perform lookup operations in your worksheet models. Table A.5 lists Excel's lookup functions.

Table A.5. Excel's Lookup and Reference Functions

Function	What It Does
ADDRESS	Calculates a reference as text to a single cell in a worksheet
AREAS	Calculates the number of areas in a reference
CHOOSE	Selects a value from a list of values
COLUMN	Calculates the column number of a reference
COLUMNS	Calculates the number of columns in a reference
FORMULATEXT	Calculates the formula at the given reference as text
GETPIVOTDATA	Calculates data stored in a PivotTable report
HLOOKUP	Looks in the top row of an array and returns the value of the indicated cell
HYPERLINK	Creates a shortcut that opens a document stored on a network or on the Internet
INDEX	Uses an index to choose a value from a reference or array
INDIRECT	Calculates a reference indicated by a text value
LOOKUP	Looks up values in a vector or array
MATCH	Looks up values in a reference or array
OFFSET	Calculates a reference offset from a given reference
ROW	Calculates the row number of a reference
ROWS	Calculates the number of rows in a reference
RTD	Retrieves real-time data from a program that supports COM automation
TRANSPOSE	Calculates the transpose of an array
VLOOKUP	Looks in the first column of an array and moves across the row to return the value of a cell

Math and Trigonometry Functions

Excel's mathematical underpinnings are revealed when you consider the long list of math-related functions that come with the program. There are functions for basic mathematical operations such as absolute values, lowest and greatest common denominators, square roots, and sums. There are also plenty of high-end operations for things like matrix multiplication, multinomials, and sums of squares. Table A.6 lists the Excel math and trigonometry functions.

Table A.6. Excel's Math and Trigonometry Functions

Function	What It Does
ABS	Calculates the absolute value of a number
ACOS	Calculates the arccosine of a number
ACOSH	Calculates the inverse hyperbolic cosine of a number
ACOT	Calculates the arccotangent of a number
ACOTH	Calculates the hyperbolic arccotangent of a number
AGGREGATE	Calculates an aggregate in a list or database
ARABIC	Converts a Roman number to Arabic, as a number
ASIN	Calculates the arcsine of a number
ASINH	Calculates the inverse hyperbolic sine of a number
ATAN	Calculates the arctangent of a number
ATAN2	Calculates the arctangent from x- and y-coordinates
ATANH	Calculates the inverse hyperbolic tangent of a number
BASE	Converts a number into a text representation with the given radix (base)
CEILING	Rounds a number to the nearest integer or to the nearest multiple of significance
CEILING.MATH	Rounds a number up, to the nearest integer or to the nearest multiple of significance
CEILING.PRECISE	Rounds a number the nearest integer or to the nearest multiple of significance. Regardless of the sign of the number, the number is rounded up.
COMBIN	Calculates the number of combinations for a given number of objects
COMBINA	Calculates the number of combinations with repetitions for a given number of items
COS	Calculates the cosine of a number
COSH	Calculates the hyperbolic cosine of a number
COT	Calculates the cotangent of an angle
COTH	Calculates the hyperbolic cotangent of a number
CSC	Calculates the cosecant of an angle
CSCH	Calculates the hyperbolic cosecant of an angle
DECIMAL	Converts a text representation of a number in a given base into a decimal number

Function	What It Does
DEGREES	Converts radians to degrees
EVEN	Rounds a number up to the nearest even integer
EXP	Calculates e raised to the power of a given number
FACT	Calculates the factorial of a number
FACTDOUBLE	Calculates the double factorial of a number
FLOOR	Rounds a number down, toward zero
FLOOR.MATH	Rounds a number down, to the nearest integer or to the nearest multiple of significance
FLOOR.PRECISE	Rounds a number down to the nearest integer or to the nearest multiple of significance. Regardless of the sign of the number, the number is rounded down.
GCD	Calculates the greatest common divisor
INT	Rounds a number down to the nearest integer
ISO.CEILING	Calculates a number that is rounded up to the nearest integer or to the nearest multiple of significance
LCM	Calculates the least common multiple
LN	Calculates the natural logarithm of a number
LOG	Calculates the logarithm of a number to a specified base
LOG10	Calculates the base-10 logarithm of a number
MDETERM	Calculates the matrix determinant of an array
MINVERSE	Calculates the matrix inverse of an array
MMULT	Calculates the matrix product of two arrays
MOD	Calculates the remainder from division
MROUND	Calculates a number rounded to the desired multiple
MULTINOMIAL	Calculates the multinomial of a set of numbers
MUNIT	Calculates the unit matrix or the specified dimension
ODD	Rounds a number up to the nearest odd integer
PI	Calculates the value of pi
POWER	Calculates the result of a number raised to a power
PRODUCT	Multiplies its arguments
QUOTIENT	Calculates the integer portion of a division
RADIANS	Converts degrees to radians

Function	What It Does
RAND	Calculates a random number between 0 and 1
RANDBETWEEN	Calculates a random number between the numbers you specify
ROMAN	Converts an Arabic numeral to Roman, as text
ROUND	Rounds a number to a specified number of digits
ROUNDDOWN	Rounds a number down, toward zero
ROUNDUP	Rounds a number up, away from zero
SEC	Calculates the secant of an angle
SECH	Calculates the hyperbolic secant of an angle
SERIESSUM	Calculates the sum of a power series based on the formula
SIGN	Calculates the sign of a number
SIN	Calculates the sine of the given angle
SINH	Calculates the hyperbolic sine of a number
SQRT	Calculates a positive square root
SQRTPI	Calculates the square root of (number * pi)
SUBTOTAL	Calculates a subtotal in a list or database
SUM	Adds its arguments
SUMIF	Adds the cells specified by a given criteria
SUMIFS	Adds the cells in a range that meet multiple criteria
SUMPRODUCT	Calculates the sum of the products of corresponding array components
SUMSQ	Calculates the sum of the squares of the arguments
SUMX2MY2	Calculates the sum of the difference of squares of corresponding values in two arrays
SUMX2PY2	Calculates the sum of the sum of squares of corresponding values in two arrays
SUMXMY2	Calculates the sum of squares of differences of corresponding values in two arrays
TAN	Calculates the tangent of a number
TANH	Calculates the hyperbolic tangent of a number
TRUNC	Truncates a number to an integer

Statistical Functions

Excel's statistical functions calculate all the standard statistical measures such as average, maximum, minimum, and standard deviation. For most of the statistical functions, you supply a list of values (called a *sample* or *population*). You can enter individual values or cells, or you can specify a range. Table A.7 lists all Excel's worksheet functions in the Statistical category.

Table A.7. Excel's Statistical Functions

Function	What It Does
AVEDEV	Calculates the average of the absolute deviations of data points from their mean
AVERAGE	Calculates the average of its arguments
AVERAGEA	Calculates the average of its arguments, including numbers, text, and logical values
AVERAGEIF	Calculates the average (arithmetic mean) of all the cells in a range that meet a given criteria
AVERAGEIFS	Calculates the average (arithmetic mean) of all cells that meet multiple criteria
BETA.DIST	Calculates the beta cumulative distribution
BETA.INV	Calculates the inverse of the cumulative distribution function for a specified beta distribution
BINOM.DIST	Calculates the individual term binomial distribution probability
BINOM.DIST.RANGE	Calculates the probability of a trial result using a binomial distribution
BINOM.INV	Calculates the smallest value for which the cumulative binomial distribution is less than or equal to a criterion value
CHISQ.DIST	Calculates the cumulative beta probability density
CHISQ.DIST.RT	Calculates the one-tailed probability of the chi-squared distribution
CHISQ.INV	Calculates the cumulative beta probability density
CHISQ.INV.RT	Calculates the inverse of the one-tailed probability of the chi-squared distribution
CHISQ.TEST	Calculates the test for independence
CONFIDENCE.NORM	Calculates the confidence interval for a population mean
CONFIDENCE.T	Calculates the confidence interval for a population mean, using a Student's t distribution
CORREL	Calculates the correlation coefficient between two data sets

Function	What It Does
COUNT	Counts how many numbers are in the list of arguments
COUNTA	Counts how many values are in the list of arguments
COUNTBLANK	Counts the number of blank cells within a range
COUNTIF	Counts the number of cells within a range that meet the given criteria
COUNTIFS	Counts the number of cells within a range that meet multiple criteria
COVARIANCE.P	Calculates covariance, the average of the products of paired deviations
COVARIANCE.S	Calculates the sample covariance, the average of the products deviations for each data point pair in two data sets
DEVSQ	Calculates the sum of squares of deviations
EXPON.DIST	Calculates the exponential distribution
F.DIST	Calculates the F probability distribution
F.DIST.RT	Calculates the right-tailed F probability distribution
F.INV	Calculates the inverse of the F probability distribution
F.INV.RT	Calculates the right-tailed inverse of the F probability distribution
F.TEST	Calculates the result of an F-test
FISHER	Calculates the Fisher transformation
FISHERINV	Calculates the inverse of the Fisher transformation
FORECAST	Calculates a value along a linear trend
FREQUENCY	Calculates a frequency distribution as a vertical array
GAMMA	Calculates the Gamma function value
GAMMA.DIST	Calculates the gamma distribution
GAMMA.INV	Calculates the inverse of the gamma cumulative distribution
GAMMALN	Calculates the natural logarithm of the gamma function, $\Gamma(x)$
GAMMALN.PRECISE	Calculates the natural logarithm of the gamma function, $\Gamma(x)$
GAUSS	Calculates 0.5 less than the standard normal cumulative distribution
GEOMEAN	Calculates the geometric mean
GROWTH	Calculates values along an exponential trend
HARMEAN	Calculates the harmonic mean
HYPGEOM.DIST	Calculates the hypergeometric distribution
INTERCEPT	Calculates the intercept of the linear regression line

Function	What It Does
KURT	Calculates the kurtosis of a data set
LARGE	Calculates the k-th largest value in a data set
LINEST	Calculates the parameters of a linear trend
LOGEST	Calculates the parameters of an exponential trend
LOGNORM.DIST	Calculates the cumulative lognormal distribution
LOGNORM.INV	Calculates the inverse of the lognormal cumulative distribution
MAX	Calculates the maximum value in a list of arguments
MAXA	Calculates the maximum value in a list of arguments, including numbers, text, and logical values
MEDIAN	Calculates the median of the given numbers
MIN	Calculates the minimum value in a list of arguments
MINA	Calculates the smallest value in a list of arguments, including numbers, text, and logical values
MODE.MULT	Calculates a vertical array of the most frequently occurring, or repetitive values in an array or range of data
MODE.SNGL	Calculates the most common value in a data set
NEGBINOM.DIST	Calculates the negative binomial distribution
NORM.DIST	Calculates the normal cumulative distribution
NORM.INV	Calculates the inverse of the normal cumulative distribution
NORM.S.DIST	Calculates the standard normal cumulative distribution
NORM.S.INV	Calculates the inverse of the standard normal cumulative distribution
PEARSON	Calculates the Pearson product moment correlation coefficient
PERCENTILE.EXC	Calculates the k-th percentile of values in a range, where k is in the range 0..1, exclusive
PERCENTILE.INC	Calculates the k-th percentile of values in a range
PERCENTRANK.EXC	Calculates the rank of a value in a data set as a percentage (0..1, exclusive) of the data set
PERCENTRANK.INC	Calculates the percentage rank of a value in a data set
PERMUT	Calculates the number of permutations for a given number of objects
PERMUTATIONA	Calculates the number of permutations for a given number of objects (with repetitions) that can be selected from the total objects
PHI	Calculates the value of the density function for a standard normal distribution

Function	What It Does
POISSON.DIST	Calculates the Poisson distribution
PROB	Calculates the probability that values in a range are between two limits
QUARTILE.EXC	Calculates the quartile of the data set, based on percentile values from 0..1, exclusive
QUARTILE.INC	Calculates the quartile of a data set
RANK.AVG	Calculates the rank of a number in a list of numbers; for values with the same rank, the average rank is returned
RANK.EQ	Calculates the rank of a number in a list of numbers; equal numbers are given the same rank
RSQ	Calculates the square of the Pearson product moment correlation coefficient
SKEW	Calculates the skewness of a distribution
SKEW.P	Calculates the skewness of a distribution based on a population: a characterization of the degree of asymmetry of a distribution around its mean
SLOPE	Calculates the slope of the linear regression line
SMALL	Calculates the k-th smallest value in a data set
STANDARDIZE	Calculates a normalized value
STDEV.P	Calculates standard deviation based on the entire population
STDEV.S	Estimates standard deviation based on a sample
STDEVA	Estimates standard deviation based on a sample, including numbers, text, and logical values
STDEVPA	Calculates standard deviation based on the entire population, including numbers, text, and logical values
STEYX	Calculates the standard error of the predicted y-value for each x in the regression
T.DIST	Calculates the Percentage Points (probability) for the Student t-distribution
T.DIST.2T	Calculates the Percentage Points (probability) for the Student t-distribution
T.DIST.RT	Calculates the Student's t-distribution
T.INV	Calculates the t-value of the Student's t-distribution as a function of the probability and the degrees of freedom
T.INV.2T	Calculates the inverse of the Student's t-distribution

Function	What It Does
T.TEST	Calculates the probability associated with a Student's t-test
TREND	Calculates values along a linear trend
TRIMMEAN	Calculates the mean of the interior of a data set
VAR.P	Calculates variance based on the entire population
VAR.S	Estimates variance based on a sample
VARA	Estimates variance based on a sample, including numbers, text, and logical values
VARPA	Calculates variance based on the entire population, including numbers, text, and logical values
WEIBULL.DIST	Calculates the Weibull distribution
Z.TEST	Calculates the one-tailed probability-value of a z-test

Engineering Functions

Excel offers quite a few functions of use to engineers. Table A.8 gives you a list of all Excel's worksheet functions in the Engineering category.

Table A.8. Excel's Engineering Functions

Function	What It Does
BESSELI	Calculates the modified Bessel function In(x)
BESSELJ	Calculates the Bessel function Jn(x)
BESSELK	Calculates the modified Bessel function Kn(x)
BESSELY	Calculates the Bessel function Yn(x)
BIN2DEC	Converts a binary number to decimal
BIN2HEX	Converts a binary number to hexadecimal
BIN2OCT	Converts a binary number to octal
BITAND	Calculates a Bitwise And of two numbers
BITLSHIFT	Calculates a value number shifted left by shift_amount bits
BITOR	Calculates a bitwise OR of two numbers
BITRSHIFT	Calculates a value number shifted right by shift_amount bits
BITXOR	Calculates a bitwise Exclusive Or of two numbers

Function	What It Does
COMPLEX	Converts real and imaginary coefficients into a complex number
CONVERT	Converts a number from one measurement system to another
DEC2BIN	Converts a decimal number to binary
DEC2HEX	Converts a decimal number to hexadecimal
DEC2OCT	Converts a decimal number to octal
DELTA	Tests whether two values are equal
ERF	Calculates the error
ERF.PRECISE	Calculates the error
ERFC	Calculates the complementary error
ERFC.PRECISE	Calculates the complementary ERF function integrated between x and infinity
GESTEP	Tests whether a number is greater than a threshold value
HEX2BIN	Converts a hexadecimal number to binary
HEX2DEC	Converts a hexadecimal number to decimal
HEX2OCT	Converts a hexadecimal number to octal
IMABS	Calculates the absolute value (modulus) of a complex number
IMAGINARY	Calculates the imaginary coefficient of a complex number
IMARGUMENT	Calculates the argument theta, an angle expressed in radians
IMCONJUGATE	Calculates the complex conjugate of a complex number
IMCOS	Calculates the cosine of a complex number
IMCOSH	Calculates the hyperbolic cosine of a complex number
IMCOT	Calculates the cotangent of a complex number
IMCSC	Calculates the cosecant of a complex number
IMCSCH	Calculates the hyperbolic cosecant of a complex number
IMDIV	Calculates the quotient of two complex numbers
IMEXP	Calculates the exponential of a complex number
IMLN	Calculates the natural logarithm of a complex number
IMLOG10	Calculates the base-10 logarithm of a complex number
IMLOG2	Calculates the base-2 logarithm of a complex number
IMPOWER	Calculates a complex number raised to an integer power
IMPRODUCT	Calculates the product of from 2 to 255 complex numbers

Function	What It Does
IMREAL	Calculates the real coefficient of a complex number
IMSEC	Calculates the secant of a complex number
IMSECH	Calculates the hyperbolic secant of a complex number
IMSIN	Calculates the sine of a complex number
IMSINH	Calculates the hyperbolic sine of a complex number
IMSQRT	Calculates the square root of a complex number
IMSUB	Calculates the difference between two complex numbers
IMSUM	Calculates the sum of complex numbers
IMTAN	Calculates the tangent of a complex number
OCT2BIN	Converts an octal number to binary
OCT2DEC	Converts an octal number to decimal
OCT2HEX	Converts an octal number to hexadecimal

Information Functions

Excel's information functions return data concerning cells, worksheets, and formula results. Table A.9 lists all the information functions.

Table A.9. Excel's Information Functions

Function	Description
CELL	Returns information about various cell attributes, including formatting, contents, and location
ERROR.TYPE	Returns a number corresponding to an error type
INFO	Returns information about the operating system and environment
ISBLANK	Returns TRUE if the value is blank
ISERR	Returns TRUE if the value is any error value except #NA
ISERROR	Returns TRUE if the value is any error value
ISEVEN	Returns TRUE if the number is even
ISLOGICAL	Returns TRUE if the value is a logical value
ISNA	Returns TRUE if the value is the #NA error value

Function	Description
ISNONTEXT	Returns TRUE if the value is not text
ISNUMBER	Returns TRUE if the value is a number
ISODD	Returns TRUE if the number is odd
ISREF	Returns TRUE if the value is a reference
ISTEXT	Returns TRUE if the value is text
N	Returns the value converted to a number (a serial number if value is a date, 1 if value is TRUE, 0 if value is any other non-numeric; note that N() exists only for compatibility with other spreadsheets and is rarely used in Excel)
NA	Returns the error value #NA
SHEET	Calculates the sheet number of the referenced sheet
SHEETS	Calculates the number of sheets in a reference
TYPE	Returns a number that indicates the data type of the value: 1 for a number, 2 for text, 4 for a logical value, 8 for a formula, 16 for an error, or 64 for an array

Database Functions

To get more control over your table analysis, you can use Excel's *database functions*. Table A.10 offers a complete list of Excel's worksheet functions in the Database category.

Table A.10. Excel's Database Functions

Function	What It Does
DAVERAGE	Calculates the average of selected database entries
DCOUNT	Counts the cells that contain numbers in a database
DCOUNTA	Counts nonblank cells in a database
DGET	Extracts from a database a single record that matches the specified criteria
DMAX	Calculates the maximum value from selected database entries
DMIN	Calculates the minimum value from selected database entries
DPRODUCT	Multiplies the values in a particular field of records that match the criteria in a database

Function	What It Does
DSTDEV	Estimates the standard deviation based on a sample of selected database entries
DSTDEVP	Calculates the standard deviation based on the entire population of selected database entries
DSUM	Adds the numbers in the field column of records in the database that match the criteria
DVAR	Estimates variance based on a sample from selected database entries
DVARP	Calculates variance based on the entire population of selected database entries

Index

 **quepublishing.com**

Browse by Topic ▼ | Browse by Format ▼ | USING | More ▼

Store | Safari Books Online

QUEPUBLISHING.COM
Your Publisher for Home & Office Computing

Quepublishing.com includes all your favorite—and some new—Que series and authors to help you learn about computers and technology for the home, office, and business.

Looking for tips and tricks, video tutorials, articles and interviews, podcasts, and resources to make your life easier? Visit **quepublishing.com**.

- **Read the latest articles and sample chapters** by Que's expert authors

- **Free podcasts** provide information on the hottest tech topics

- **Register your Que products** and receive updates, supplemental content, and a coupon to be used on your next purchase

- **Check out promotions and special offers** available from Que and our retail partners

- **Join the site** and receive members-only offers and benefits

QUE NEWSLETTER
quepublishing.com/newslette

 twitter.com/ quepublishing

 facebook.com/ quepublishing

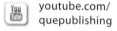 youtube.com/ quepublishing

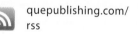 quepublishing.com/ rss

CHECK OUT MUST-HAVE BOOKS IN THE BESTSELLING MY...SERIES

Full-Color, Step-by-Step Guides

The "My..." series is a visually rich, task-based series to help you get up and running with your new device and technology and tap into some of the hidden, or less obvious features. The organized, task-based format allows you to quickly and easily find exactly the task you want to accomplish, and then shows you how to achieve it with minimal text and plenty of visual cues.

**Visit quepublishing.com/mybooks to learn more
about the My... book series from Que.**

Your purchase of **My Office® for iPad®** includes access to a free online edition for 45 days through the **Safari Books Online** subscription service. Nearly every Que book is available online through **Safari Books Online**, along with thousands of books and videos from publishers such as Addison-Wesley Professional, Cisco Press, Exam Cram, IBM Press, O'Reilly Media, Prentice Hall.

Safari Books Onli   thousands
of technology, digita   eading
publishers. With on   to learning
tools and informati   and tricks
on using your favor   much more.

STEP 1:

STEP 2:

If

Addison
Wesley

Adobe Pre

Peachpit
Press

PRENTICE
HALL

O'REILLY

wrox